30 minute
LOW-FAT

30 minute
LOW-FAT

contents

All the recipes in this book can be prepared and cooked in under 30 minutes. Some recipes may require a little additional standing or cooling time to reach perfection, but the hard work can be done in 30 minutes or less. Every one of these recipes contains less than 5 grams of fat per serving.

introduction

For most of us, today's lifestyle can only be described as frantic and chaotic, as we try to juggle work, family, household chores and life in general. Getting the balance right is often the biggest struggle and we frequently turn to shortcuts, to try and ease the pressure. After stressful, busy days at work, many of us arrive home having to cook dinner, which is often a chore, resulting in a reliance on unhealthy shortcuts and ready meals.

With a little bit of planning and forward thinking, the chore of cooking, and more importantly low-fat cooking, can be achieved and maintained with positive results. By simply sitting down once a week and menu planning the meals for the week ahead, and writing a definitive list of ingredients, you will not only save time, but money as well.

The key to low-fat cooking is using fresh, good quality ingredients, prepared using simple, quick cooking techniques. Try to purchase your meat from a good quality butcher, where freshness and superior quality are guaranteed. Always buy seafood from a reputable fishmonger, whose premises appear and smell clean. When buying fruit and vegetables, try and buy seasonally from markets and greengrocers, where freshness and quality are ensured.

The recipes in this book have been selected to demonstrate just how quick and easy low-fat meals can be to produce and how they can become an exciting and nutritious part of everyday cooking. With the abundance of fresh ingredients available to us today, there are no excuses for not living a healthy balanced lifestyle, and these recipes are great low-fat options to help you achieve this. So get organised, plan your meals and start enjoying the benefits of low-fat eating.

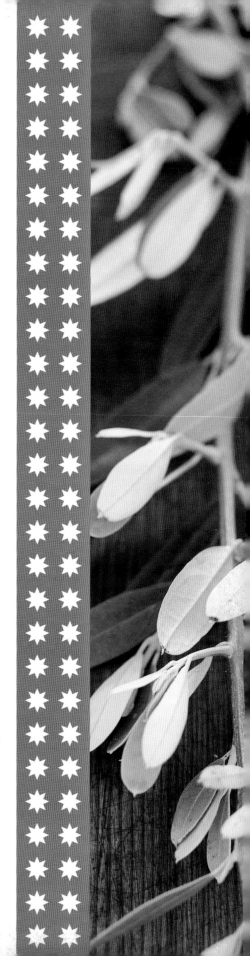

starters

People often think that low-fat cooking means you have to go without and, therefore, three courses are out of the question. We all love to entertain, whether it be a casual barbecue with friends or a smart dinner party. The following recipes are packed full of flavour; they look impressive, take less than 30 minutes to cook and, most importantly, are low-fat.

The importance of the first course, whether you serve an uncomplicated spread such as broad bean dip with plain toast, a smooth home-made fish pâté or a refreshing gazpacho soup, is paramount. It sets the stage for what is to follow and must balance perfectly with the main and dessert courses. The starter sets the tone for the rest of the meal — open with a sensational starter and your guests will sit expectantly at your table, happily anticipating what is to follow.

The recipes featured in this chapter provide a wonderful selection of flavoursome low-fat dishes and showcase the variety of cooking methods, flavours and ingredients that are available to us today from around the world. Impress your friends with the classic French starter of artichokes vinaigrette, or make it a hands-on affair with everyone around the table involved in making Vietnamese rice paper rolls.

The importance of fresh produce is demonstrated throughout these recipes, with vegetables and seafood being the key ingredients. Popular low-fat cooking methods like poaching and griddling are also used prevalently throughout these recipes.

For those of you looking for a light lunch or a fresh simple evening meal, try the moules mariniéres, the smoked tuna and white bean salad with basil dressing, or the delicious octopus salad. When you find tomatoes at their best, make sure to try the tasty gazpacho recipe — you'll love it!

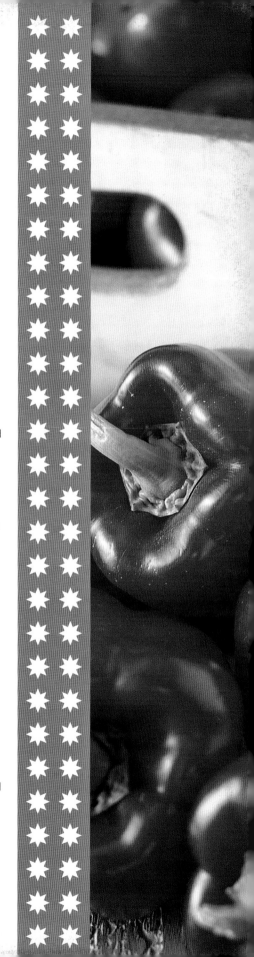

Gazpacho

SERVES 4 ∗ PREPARATION TIME: 15 MINUTES ∗ COOKING TIME: NIL

The Spanish have devised many ways to deal with the searing heat of their summers, not the least of them, the cold soup. Gazpacho, the most famous of these wonderfully refreshing soups, is simplicity itself to make — and even easier to eat.

1 kg (2 lb 4 oz) vine-ripened
   tomatoes
2 slices day-old white crusty bread,
   crusts removed and broken
   into pieces
1 red pepper (capsicum), seeded
   and roughly chopped
2 garlic cloves, chopped
1 small green chilli, chopped,
   optional
1 teaspoon sugar
2 tablespoons red wine vinegar
2 tablespoons extra virgin olive oil

Garnish
½ Lebanese (short) cucumber,
   seeded and finely diced
½ red pepper (capsicum), seeded
   and finely diced
½ green pepper (capsicum), seeded
   and finely diced
½ red onion, finely diced
½ vine-ripened tomato, diced

1. Score a cross in the base of each tomato. Put in a bowl of boiling water for 10 seconds, then plunge into cold water and peel away the skin from the cross. Cut the tomatoes in half and scoop out the seeds with a teaspoon. Chop the tomato flesh.

2. Soak the bread in cold water for 5 minutes, then squeeze out any excess liquid. Put the bread in a food processor with the tomato, peppers, garlic, chilli, sugar and red wine vinegar and process until combined and smooth.

3. With the motor running, add the oil to make a smooth, creamy mixture. Season to taste. Refrigerate for at least 2 hours. Add a little extra vinegar, if desired.

4. To make the garnish, mix together the ingredients. Spoon the chilled gazpacho into soup bowls, top with a little of the garnish and serve the remaining garnish in separate bowls on the side to add as desired.

Soak the bread briefly in water, then squeeze out excess liquid.

Prepare the cucumber for the garnish by seeding it, then dicing.

Sweet potato salad with orange-sesame dressing

SERVES 4 * **PREPARATION TIME: 15 MINUTES** * **COOKING TIME: 15 MINUTES**

Sweet potato and orange are one of those food combinations that are just meant to go together. Roasting or grilling sweet potato makes it tender and enhances its sweetness. This salad, with its contrast of sweet and tangy, soft and crisp, is easy but impressive.

1 pitta bread
olive oil spray for cooking
500 g (1 lb 2 oz) orange sweet
    potato, unpeeled, cut into slices
    1 cm (½ inch) thick
1 small orange
150 g (5½ oz) baby spinach

Dressing
3 tablespoons olive oil
1 teaspoon sesame oil
2 tablespoons orange juice
1 teaspoon lemon juice
1 teaspoon finely grated
    orange zest
1 garlic clove, crushed
2 teaspoons dijon mustard

1. Preheat a grill (broiler) to high. Cut off and discard the edge of the pitta bread, split the bread into 2 thin halves, and lightly spray with oil. Place under the grill and toast until crisp and lightly browned. Reserve.

2. Lightly spray the sweet potato with oil and grill until soft and golden on both sides for 8–10 minutes. Transfer to a salad bowl.

3. Peel the orange, removing all the pith. To fillet the segments, hold the orange over a bowl and use a sharp knife to cut down either side of the membranes. Put the segments in the bowl and add the spinach. Break up the pitta crisps into small shards and put into the bowl. Toss lightly.

4. To make the dressing, put all the ingredients in a small bowl and whisk to blend. Season with salt and freshly ground black pepper, to taste. Pour over the salad just before serving.

Cut off the edge of the pitta bread, then split in half

Cut the orange segments away from the membrane

17 mins

Crab, cucumber and wakame salad

SERVES 4 ✳ **PREPARATION TIME: 15 MINUTES** ✳ **COOKING TIME: 2 MINUTES**

This appealingly fresh summer salad combines three contrasting textures of crab, cucumber and seaweed. The light dressing, which, like most Japanese dressings, dilutes the vinegar with dashi rather than oil, enhances the natural flavours of the ingredients while never overpowering them.

2 Lebanese (short) cucumbers
2 tablespoons dried wakame
  seaweed pieces
150 g (5½ oz/1 cup) fresh
  crabmeat, cooked and picked over
  (or good-quality tinned crabmeat)

Dressing
2 tablespoons Japanese
  rice vinegar
½ teaspoon dashi granules
1 tablespoon shoyu (Japanese
  soy sauce)
2 teaspoons mirin
20 g (¾ oz) fresh ginger

Note: 1 regular cucumber may be used in place of 2 Lebanese (short) cucumbers.

1. Dissolve 2 teaspoons salt in 500 ml (17 fl oz/2 cups) cold water. Cut the cucumbers in half lengthways, scoop out the seeds, then slice the flesh very thinly. Put the cucumber flesh in the cold water and soak for 10 minutes. Drain well and squeeze out any excess moisture. Keep in the refrigerator until needed.

2. Soak the wakame in a bowl of cold water for 5 minutes, or until rehydrated and glossy but not mushy. Drain well, then refrigerate until needed.

3. To make the dressing, combine the rice vinegar, dashi granules, shoyu and mirin with 2 tablespoons water in a small saucepan and bring to the boil over high heat. Remove from the heat and cool to room temperature. Finely grate the ginger, then squeeze the grated ginger with your fingertips to release the juice (you will need 1½ teaspoons of ginger juice). Add the ginger juice to the dressing and stir well. Allow to cool completely. Refrigerate for 15 minutes, or until cold.

4. Neatly arrange the cucumber, wakame and crabmeat in four small serving dishes, then carefully pour the dressing over the top.

Halve the cucumbers lengthways, scoop out the seeds and slice

Soak the cucumber slices in cold salted water for 10 minutes

Artichokes vinaigrette

SERVES 4 * **PREPARATION TIME: 5 MINUTES** * **COOKING TIME: 25 MINUTES**

The French understand that fine produce just needs some careful preparation and understated embellishing to shine as here, with this classic presentation for artichokes. Use the best olive oil and vinegar you can find and choose firm, compact artichokes with tight leaves.

1 lemon, juiced
4 globe artichokes

Vinaigrette
100 ml (3½ fl oz) olive oil
2 spring onions (scallions),
    finely chopped
2 tablespoons white wine
2 tablespoons white wine vinegar
¼ teaspoon dijon mustard
a pinch sugar
1 tablespoon finely chopped
    flat-leaf (Italian) parsley

1. To prepare the artichokes, bring a large saucepan of salted water to the boil and add the lemon juice. Break the stalks from the artichokes, pulling out any strings at the same time. Remove the tough outer leaves and then trim the bases flat. Add the artichokes to the water and put a small plate on top of them to keep them submerged. Cook at a simmer for 20-30 minutes, or until a leaf from the base comes away easily. (The base will be tender when pierced with a skewer.) Cool under cold running water, then drain upside down on a tray.

2. To make the vinaigrette, heat 1 tablespoon of the oil in a small saucepan, add the spring onion and cook over low heat for 2 minutes. Leave to cool a little, then add the white wine, vinegar, mustard and sugar and gradually whisk in the remaining oil. Season well with salt and pepper and stir in half the parsley.

3. Place an artichoke on each plate and gently prise it open a little. Spoon the dressing over the top, allowing it to drizzle into the artichoke and around the plate. Pour the remaining dressing into a bowl for dipping the leaves. Sprinkle each artichoke with parsley.

4. Eat the leaves one by one, dipping them in the vinaigrette and pulling the flesh off the leaves between your teeth. When you reach the middle, pull off any really small leaves and then use a teaspoon to remove the furry choke. Once you've got rid of the choke, you can eat the tender base, or heart, of the artichoke.

Trim off the outer leaves then cut the bases so they are flat.

Whisk the wine, vinegar, mustard, sugar and oil into the mixture.

23 mins

Vietnamese cucumber salad with steamed fish

SERVES 4 * **PREPARATION TIME: 15 MINUTES + MARINATING TIME**
COOKING TIME: 8 MINUTES

Steaming fish, whether whole or in slices, is a common cooking method in Asia. A crisp, refreshing salad with a sour-sweet dressing is a perfect complement. Haddock, monkfish and hake are suitable substitutes for the cod in this recipe.

Salad

1 teaspoon lime juice
2 tablespoons sweet chilli sauce
1–2 tablespoons fish sauce
½–1 tablespoon grated palm sugar
  (or raw caster (superfine) sugar)
4 Lebanese (short) cucumbers,
  cut into 2 cm (¾ inch) chunks
½ red onion, sliced
1 large pear
1 small handful Vietnamese mint
1 small handful Thai basil

2 lemon grass stems, trimmed
  and finely chopped
80 ml (2½ fl oz/⅓ cup) fish sauce
50 g (1¾ oz/¼ cup) grated
  palm sugar (or raw caster
  (superfine) sugar)
1 kg (2 lb 4 oz) cod fillets
80 g (2¾ oz/½ cup) chopped
  roasted unsalted peanuts

Note: 2 regular cucumbers may be used in place of 4 Lebanese (short) cucumbers.

1. To make the salad, combine the lime juice and sweet chilli sauce in a large bowl and add the fish sauce and palm sugar, to taste. Add the cucumber and onion. Quarter and core the pear, slice it thinly and add it to the bowl. Chop half the mint and basil leaves, add to the bowl and toss to coat. Cover and set aside in a cool place for 2 hours.

2. Meanwhile, combine the lemon grass, fish sauce and palm sugar in a large bowl. Slice the cod into 1 cm (½ inch) thick slices and add to the bowl. Toss to coat, cover with plastic wrap and chill for 1 hour.

3. Line a large bamboo steamer with baking paper and cover with as many slices of cod as will fit in a single layer. Place over a wok or saucepan of boiling water and steam for 4 minutes, or until cooked through. Repeat with the remaining fish.

4. To serve, toss the remaining mint leaves and the peanuts through the salad. Divide among 4 serving plates and top with the fish and the remaining basil leaves.

Quarter and core the pear, then slice it thinly

Steam fish in a single layer in a steamer lined with baking paper

Calamares a la plancha

SERVES 6 ✳ **PREPARATION TIME: 15 MINUTES + STANDING TIME**
COOKING TIME: 5 MINUTES

'A la plancha' means cooking on a hot flat plate, as opposed to 'a la parilla', which means on the grill. A la plancha is a favourite method in many tapas bars, and calamari prepared this way — sweet and tender, slightly charred and sprinkled with parsley and garlic — are especially good.

500 g (1 lb 2 oz) small squid
olive oil spray for cooking

Parsley dressing
2 tablespoons extra virgin olive oil
2 tablespoons finely chopped
   flat-leaf (Italian) parsley
1 garlic clove, crushed

To prepare the squid, first pull the tentacles away from the hood.

Cut under the eyes and reserve the tentacles. Grasp the soft bone in the hood and pull out. Discard.

1. To clean the squid, gently pull the tentacles away from the hood (the intestines should come away at the same time). Remove the intestines from the tentacles by cutting under the eyes, then remove the beak if it remains in the centre of the tentacles by using your fingers to push up the centre. Discard the beak. Pull away the soft bone from the hood.

2. Rub the hoods under cold running water. The skin should come away easily. Wash the hoods and tentacles and drain well. Transfer to a bowl, add ¼ teaspoon salt and mix well. Cover and refrigerate for 30 minutes.

3. Just before cooking, whisk the dressing ingredients with some salt and ¼ teaspoon freshly ground black pepper in a jug or bowl.

4. Lightly spray the oil in a frying pan over high heat and cook the squid hoods in small batches for 2–3 minutes, or until the hoods turn white and are tender. Cook the squid tentacles, turning to brown them all over, for 1 minute, or until they curl up. Serve hot, drizzled with the parsley dressing.

Three ways with beetroot

For those who know beetroot only from jars, trying the fresh variety will open your eyes to a whole new world. The depth of flavour contained in these scarlet globes can only be captured if you start with a suede-skinned raw beetroot. Baby beets are the sweetest and are perfect with tatsoi and a sweet-tangy dressing. Roasting them with a whole bulb of garlic adds a smoky depth, or try this zesty citrus glaze to complement and yet cut through the sweetness at the same time.

Baby beetroot and tatsoi salad

SERVES 4 ✳ **PREPARATION TIME: 15 MINUTES** ✳ **COOKING TIME: 10 MINUTES**

Wearing rubber gloves, trim 1.6 kg (3 lb 8 oz/2 bunches) baby beetroot, discarding the stalks but reserving the unblemished leaves. Bring a medium saucepan of water to the boil. Add the beetroot and simmer, covered, for 8–10 minutes, or until tender, then drain. Ease off the skins, pat dry with paper towels and rinse. Put the beetroot in a large shallow bowl. Bring a small saucepan of water to the boil. Add a large pinch of salt and 250 g (9 oz/12/3 cups) broad (fava) beans (from 500 g (1 lb 2 oz/3 cups) fresh broad beans in the pod) and simmer for 2–3 minutes, then drain. When cool enough to handle, slip the beans out of their skins and add to the beetroot. Add the reserved beetroot leaves and the small inner leaves of 200 g (7 oz/1 bunch) tatsoi (pak choi or choi sum may also be used). To make the dressing, put 80 ml (2½ fl oz/⅓ cup) olive oil and 1 tablespoon each of lemon juice, wholegrain mustard and honey in a small bowl and whisk well to combine. Season with salt and freshly ground black pepper, to taste. Pour over the beetroot mixture and toss gently. Serve warm or at room temperature.

Roasted beetroot and whole garlic

SERVES 4 ✳ **PREPARATION TIME: 10 MINUTES** ✳ **COOKING TIME: 15 MINUTES**

Line a roasting tin with baking paper. Cut 250 g (9 oz) of pre-cooked beetroot into quarters. Combine 1 tablespoon balsamic vinegar and 100 ml (3½ fl oz) olive oil and drizzle. Season lightly with salt and freshly ground black pepper. Wrap the beetroot in foil with 12 cloves of garlic and drizzle over half the dressing. Roast in a preheated 200°C (400°F/Gas 6) oven for 15-20 minutes, or until the beetroot is tender. Unwrap and gently squeeze the garlic flesh out from 1 clove. Add to the remaining dressing and mix in with a fork. Transfer the beetroot to a serving dish and drizzle with the garlic dressing. Scatter the remaining garlic cloves around and serve immediately.

Orange-glazed beetroot with dill

SERVES 4 ✳ **PREPARATION TIME: 10 MINUTES** ✳ **COOKING TIME: 20 MINUTES**

Wearing rubber gloves, trim 750 g (1 lb 10 oz) small beetroot and put in a large saucepan of cold water. Cover and bring to the boil over high heat. Reduce the heat to medium and simmer, partly covered, for 10 minutes, or until tender, then drain. Meanwhile, heat 1 tablespoon olive oil in a large frying pan. Add 1 teaspoon each of dill seeds and ground cumin and stir over medium heat for 20–25 seconds, or until aromatic. Add 250 ml (9 fl oz/1 cup) orange juice, increase the heat and boil for 5–6 minutes, or until reduced by half. Peel the beetroot, then cut each into 4 wedges. Add to the frying pan and cook, stirring often, for 2–3 minutes. Stir in 2 teaspoons chopped dill and the grated zest of half a small orange. Serve hot or at room temperature.

Fresh spring rolls

MAKES 8 * **PREPARATION TIME: 20 MINUTES** * **COOKING TIME: 5 MINUTES**

Fun to make, with a minimum of cooking, these fresh spring rolls can be prepared 2–3 hours in advance and left at room temperature, covered with damp paper towels. Alternatively, set out small bowls of each ingredient on the table and let diners assemble their own.

Dipping sauce
1 tablespoon fish sauce
1 teaspoon grated palm sugar
1 tablespoon lime juice
2 tablespoons finely chopped coriander (cilantro) leaves
1 red bird's eye chilli, finely chopped

50 g (1¾ oz) dried rice vermicelli
2 spring onions (scallions)
30 g (1 oz) mangetout (snow peas), topped and tailed
½ Lebanese (short) cucumber
2 (about 150 g/5½ oz) baby pak choy (bok choy)
1 tablespoon oil
1 garlic clove, crushed
½ teaspoon finely grated fresh ginger
8 round rice paper wrappers, each 16 cm (6¼ inches) in diameter
30 g (1 oz/⅓ cup) bean sprouts, tailed
1 small handful coriander (cilantro) leaves
60 ml (2 fl oz/¼ cup) hoisin sauce

Note: ¼ regular cucumber may be used in place of ½ Lebanese (short) cucumber.

1. To make the dipping sauce, combine the fish sauce, palm sugar, lime juice and 2 tablespoons water in a small bow. Stir until the sugar has dissolved. Add the coriander and chilli and set aside. Soak the vermicelli in hot water for 10 minutes, then drain.

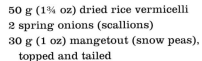

2. Cut the spring onions into 7–8 cm (2¾–3¼ inch) lengths and shred them lengthways. Shred the mangetout lengthways. Cut the cucumber into 7–8 cm (2¾–3¼ inch) matchsticks.

3. Discard the outer leaves of the pak choy. Cut off the bases and separate the leaves. Heat the oil in a wok over medium–high heat and fry the garlic and ginger for 10–15 seconds, until aromatic. Add the pak choy and stir-fry for 20–30 seconds, or until wilted. Remove from the heat and cut lengthways into thin slices.

4. Soak a rice paper wrapper in lukewarm water just until soft. Spread a dry tea towel on a work surface and put the rice paper wrapper on top. Arrange a small bunch of vermicelli on one side. Top with 3–4 lengths of pak choy. Cover with 2–3 bean sprouts, slightly protruding over the rim of the wrapper. Add 2–3 mangetout strips, some spring onion and some cucumber sticks. Put 2 coriander leaves on top and spoon a thin trail of hoisin sauce along the length of the vegetables.

5. Fold the bottom of the wrapper up over the vegetables, then roll the wrapper up tightly from one side to give a firm cigar shape with a few vegetable sprigs sticking out the top. Repeat with the remaining ingredients to make 8 rolls. Serve with dipping sauce.

Spoon a drizzle of hoisin sauce over the vegetables

Fold up the bottom of the rice paper wrapper, then the sides

22 mins

Broad bean dip

SERVES 6 * **PREPARATION TIME: 20 MINUTES** * **COOKING TIME: 2 MINUTES**

Known as bessara in Morocco, this dip can also be made into a soup. Cook until the beans are tender, purée the beans and return them to the pan with the remaining ingredients. Add water to give a thick soup consistency. Heat until boiling and serve sprinkled with chopped parsley, paprika and cumin.

500 g (1 lb 2 oz/2 cup) frozen
    broad (fava) beans, thawed
2 garlic cloves, crushed
½ teaspoon ground cumin
1½ tablespoons lemon juice
up to 80 ml (2½ fl oz/⅓ cup)
    olive oil
a large pinch paprika
2 tablespoons chopped flat-leaf
    (Italian) parsley
flat bread to serve

1. Drain the beans. Remove the skin (slit the skin with the point of a knife and slip out the bean). Put the beans in a large saucepan of boiling water, cook for 2 minutes. Drain the beans, allow to cool.

2. Purée the beans in a food processor, then transfer to a bowl and stir in the garlic, cumin and lemon juice. Add salt, to taste. Gradually stir in enough oil to give a spreadable or thick dipping consistency. If the mixture thickens as it cools, stir through a little warm water. Spread the bean purée over a large dish and sprinkle the paprika and parsley over the top. Serve with the flat bread.

broad beans

Broad beans, also known as fava beans, have been a staple food of the region for millennia — especially the dried beans, as they keep for many months. These require lengthy soaking so that the leathery skin can be removed, which results in the best flavour and a creamy white purée. Because this is time consuming, it is possible to purchase ready-skinned dried broad beans at Middle Eastern markets that only require overnight soaking. Fresh broad beans are used when in season, the young beans added to tagines with the skin on; when more mature, the beans are blanched and skinned before cooking.

Cucumber and radish salsa with crisp-skinned salmon

SERVES 4 ❋ **PREPARATION TIME: 15 MINUTES** ❋ **COOKING TIME: 5 MINUTES**

Radishes are peppery root vegetables related to the mustard plant. There are many varieties, which may be red, black or white (daikon). Buy smooth, firm, small radishes; large ones tend to be tough. Store them without their leaves, as these accelerate moisture loss.

Salsa
1 large cucumber
2 celery stalks, thinly sliced
1 French shallot, diced
1 avocado, diced
20 baby white and/or red radishes, halved, or quartered if large
1 small handful coriander (cilantro)

Dressing
80 ml (2½ fl oz/⅓ cup) olive oil
2 tablespoons lime juice
1 teaspoon finely grated lime zest
1 garlic clove, crushed
1 teaspoon honey

Add the salmon, skin side down, to the frying pan

4 small salmon fillets, skin on
olive oil spray for pan-frying
1 small handful coriander (cilantro)

1. To make the salsa, peel the cucumber and cut in half lengthways. Using a teaspoon, scoop out and discard the seeds. Slice very thinly into half-moon shapes and put in a large bowl. Add the celery, shallot, avocado, radishes and coriander.

2. To make the dressing, put the oil, lime juice, lime zest, garlic and honey in a small bowl and mix well. Season with salt and freshly ground black pepper, to taste.

3. Sprinkle the salmon skin with a little salt. Lightly spray oil in a large frying pan over high heat. When hot, add the salmon, skin side down, and immediately hold a spatula or another frying pan on top of the fillets to keep them flat. Fry for 1–2 minutes, or until the skin is crisp and brown all over. Reduce the heat to medium and turn the salmon. Cook until just opaque, 2–3 minutes, depending on the thickness. Drain on paper towels.

4. When cool enough to handle, use kitchen scissors to cut each salmon fillet across the grain into 3 strips. Break each strip into bite-sized pieces of several flakes. Add to the salsa, along with the dressing and coriander. Toss gently to coat, and serve immediately.

Using kitchen scissors, cut the salmon into strips

30 mins

Moroccan fish soup

SERVES 6 ✳ **PREPARATION TIME: 15 MINUTES** ✳ **COOKING TIME: 15 MINUTES**

With such a variety of fish available, it is surprising that there are so few fish soup recipes in Moroccan cooking. This soup is typical of the cuisine in Tetuán, in the country's north, where Spanish influences still prevail.

2 roasted red peppers (capsicums)
1 long red chilli
1 tablespoon extra virgin olive oil
1 onion, finely chopped
1 tablespoon tomato purée (paste)
2–3 teaspoons harissa, to taste
4 garlic cloves, finely chopped
2 teaspoons ground cumin
750 ml (26 fl oz/3 cups) fish stock
400 g (14 oz) tinned crushed
   tomatoes
750 g (1 lb 10 oz) firm white fish,
   such as blue eye cod or ling,
   cut into 2 cm (¾ in) cubes
2 bay leaves
2 tablespoons chopped coriander
   (cilantro) leaves

1. Heat the oil in a large saucepan and cook the onion for 5 minutes, or until softened. Stir in the tomato purée, harissa, garlic, cumin and 125 ml (4 fl oz/½ cup) water. Add the stock, tomatoes and 500 ml (17 fl oz/2 cups) water. Bring to the boil, then reduce the heat and add the fish and bay leaves. Simmer for 7–8 minutes.

2. Remove the fish and discard the bay leaves. When the soup has cooled slightly, add half the coriander and purée until smooth. Season with salt and pepper. Return the soup to the pan, add the fish, peppers and chilli and simmer gently for 5 minutes. Garnish with the remaining coriander and serve hot with crusty bread.

cumin

Used from antiquity in the Middle East, cumin was introduced into Morocco by the Arabs and has become one of the most popular spices, used in fish and chicken tagines and soups, and mixed with salt and sprinkled on kebabs and hard-boiled eggs. It is essential for mechoui (slow-roasted lamb). Many Moroccan cooks prefer to freshly pound cumin seeds to attain maximum flavour. A darker cumin — greenish-brown in colour — is the one to choose, as lighter cumin could be mixed with ground coriander seeds. It should have an oily feel between the fingers with a warm and sweet, yet pungent and earthy, aroma.

Summer salad of mixed salad greens, mango, avocado and prawns

SERVES 4 ∗ **PREPARATION TIME: 15 MINUTES** ∗ **COOKING TIME: 5 MINUTES**

Avocados have soft, buttery flesh, a mild, slightly nutty flavour, and skins that may be smooth or rough. Cut avocado turns brown, so cut it just before use or brush it with lemon juice to prevent discolouration. Firm, unripe avocados will ripen at room temperature after 3–4 days.

lettuce

Long gone are the days when lettuce meant iceberg and only iceberg. An extensive range of fresh lettuces is now available. Some of the varieties so differ in taste and texture that it seems the name is all that they have in common. Whether soft, leafy, crisp or bitter, any and all of these lettuces make a fabulous salad alone or tossed together. Lettuce is at its best in summer and should be stored either in a lettuce crisper or wrapped in a damp tea-towel in the fridge. Wash thoroughly and dry well, using paper towels, tea towels, or a salad spinner; any moisture left on the leaves will dilute the dressing. A quick soak in cold water can revive slightly limp leaves, but extensive soaking will cause them to lose flavour.

Dressing
80 ml (2½ fl oz/⅓ cup) olive oil
1 tablespoon white wine vinegar
1 tablespoon dijon mustard
1 teaspoon grated orange zest

24 (about 600 g/1 lb 5 oz) raw
   medium prawns (shrimp), peeled
   and deveined, tails intact
1 small red onion
2 avocados
2 mangoes
1 baby cos (romaine) lettuce
½ red oakleaf lettuce
½ butter lettuce

1. To make the dressing, put the olive oil, vinegar, mustard and orange zest in a small bowl and mix well. Season with salt and freshly ground black pepper, to taste.

2. Preheat a barbecue or griddle pan to medium heat. Lightly brush the prawns with a little of the dressing, arrange on the grill plate or pan and cook for 5 minutes, or until crisp and opaque. Transfer to a large bowl.

3. Finely slice the onion lengthways and add to the bowl. Slice the avocados into large wedges and add to the bowl. Slice the cheeks off the mangoes and peel them. Cut into slices and add to the bowl.

4. Discard the damaged outer leaves of the lettuces and tear the leaves into smaller pieces. Add to the bowl. Pour in the dressing and toss lightly before serving.

Three ways with fish pâté

These recipes use different types of smoked fish. Smoked foods are first treated with either brine or dry salt, then smoked over smouldering sawdust. The wood used helps determine the flavour of the finished product. There are two methods of smoking. Cold smoking flavours the food without cooking it; such foods generally need to be cooked before they are eaten, smoked salmon being an exception. Hot smoking cooks the food while also imparting a delicious smoky flavour.

Smoked trout pâté

SERVES 6 ✳ **PREPARATION TIME: 10 MINUTES** ✳ **COOKING TIME: NIL**

Skin 2 whole smoked trout, remove the heads, then lift the flesh off the bones. Alternatively, use 4 skinned smoked trout fillets. Break the flesh into flakes and put in a bowl or food processor. Either mash the flesh with a fork or briefly process until it is broken up, but still with plenty of texture. Beat 200 g (7 oz) low-fat cream cheese with a wooden spoon until soft. Add the smoked trout flesh and mix together well. Stir in 2 tablespoons finely chopped dill and the juice of half a lemon. Season with salt, freshly ground black pepper and a pinch of cayenne pepper. Chill the pâté until you need it, but bring it to room temperature before serving. Serve with toasted slices of baguette, melba toast, or triangles of brown toast with the crusts removed. Provide extra lemon wedges to squeeze over.

Smoked salmon pâté

SERVES 4–6 ✳ **PREPARATION TIME: 10 MINUTES** ✳ **COOKING TIME: NIL**

Put 2 tablespoons rinsed, dried and roughly chopped capers and 1 seeded and finely chopped small red chilli in a food processor. Add 100 g (3½ oz) smoked salmon (trimmings are fine) and blend for about 10 seconds. Add 200 g (7 oz) quark and blend until smooth. Add 3–4 tablespoons half fat crème fraiche, depending on how thick the pâté is, and blend again. Transfer to a bowl and add 1 tablespoon finely chopped flat-leaf (Italian) parsley and 1–2 tablespoons lemon juice, to taste. Season with salt and freshly ground black pepper and refrigerate until needed. Serve with melba toast or triangles of brown toast with the crusts removed.

Smoked mackerel pâté

SERVES 4–6 ✳ **PREPARATION TIME: 10 MINUTES** ✳ **COOKING TIME: NIL**

Remove the skin from 225 g (8 oz) peppered smoked mackerel fillets (about 2 fillets). Put them in a bowl and mash with a fork. Add 80 g (2¾ oz) light sour cream, 1 tablespoon creamed horseradish and 2 tablespoons lime juice. Mix everything together well, season with a little salt if needed, then refrigerate until ready to use. Serve with melba toast or triangles of brown toast with the crusts removed. This also makes a great sandwich filling with watercress.

23 mins

Octopus salad

SERVES 4 * **PREPARATION TIME: 15 MINUTES + MARINATING TIME** *
COOKING TIME: 8 MINUTES

Many recipes for octopus come from Mediterranean countries, where this cephalopod is plentiful. This recipe combines tender simmered octopus with typical Mediterranean flavours to produce a simple salad, perfect for a summer lunch.

650 g (1 lb 7 oz) baby octopus, cleaned
120 g (4¼ oz) mixed salad leaves
lemon wedges to serve

Dressing
2 tablespoons lemon juice
100 ml (3½ fl oz) olive oil
1 garlic clove, thinly sliced
1 tablespoon chopped mint
1 tablespoon chopped flat-leaf (Italian) parsley
1 teaspoon dijon mustard
a pinch cayenne pepper

1. Bring a large saucepan of water to the boil and add the octopus. Simmer for 8–10 minutes, or until the octopus is tender when tested with the point of a knife.

2. Meanwhile, make the dressing by mixing together the lemon juice, olive oil, garlic, mint, parsley, mustard and cayenne pepper with some salt and freshly ground black pepper.

3. Drain the octopus well and put in a bowl. Pour the dressing over the top and cool for a few minutes before transferring to the refrigerator. Chill for at least 3 hours before serving on a bed of salad leaves. Drizzle a little of the dressing over the top and serve with lemon wedges.

octopus

The octopus has more often filled our imaginations than our stomachs. One species can grow to 10 m (30 ft) from head to tentacle-tip and scientists have proven that octopuses are intelligent, with long- and short-term memories. So, perhaps it is not entirely surprising that many cooks are happier with baby octopus. Apart from size, the main difference between baby octopus and larger ones is the tenderness of the former; it needs neither beating nor blanching before cooking. Baby octopus can be cooked whole and are perfect for barbecuing and adding to salads. Japanese and Mediterranean cooks in particular make excellent use of these tender creatures.

Roasted pepper, chilli and semi-dried tomato spread

SERVES 4 ✳ **PREPARATION TIME: 10 MINUTES** ✳ **COOKING TIME: 10 MINUTES**

Serve this spread with crudites, toasted Turkish bread fingers or other breads and crackers. It also goes well with boiled new potatoes. Store the spread, covered, in the refrigerator for up to 5 days.

1 large red pepper (capsicum),
  quartered and seeded
90 g (3¼ oz/2/3 cup) semi-dried
  (sun-blushed) tomatoes
2 teaspoons sambal oelek
125 g (4½ oz/½ cup) spreadable
  light cream cheese
2 tablespoons chopped basil

Note: Sambal oelek is available in good supermarkets, Asian and Thai grocers. Chilli paste may be used as a substitute for sambal oelek in this recipe.

1. Preheat the grill (broiler) to high. Arrange the pepper, skin side up, on the grill rack and grill (broil) for 10 minutes, or until well blackened. Cool in a plastic bag, then peel and discard the skin. Chop the flesh.

2. Drain the tomatoes well on paper towels, pat dry and roughly chop. Put in a small food processor fitted with the metal blade and add the pepper, sambal oelek, cream cheese and basil. Whizz for 10 seconds, or until roughly combined. The tomatoes should still have some texture. Season well with salt and freshly ground black pepper.

Peel away and discard the skin from the roasted pepper

Put all the ingredients in the bowl of a food processor. Process until coarsely chopped but still retaining some texture

10 mins

Smoked tuna and white bean salad with basil dressing

SERVES 4 ✳ PREPARATION TIME: 10 MINUTES ✳ COOKING TIME: NIL

Tinned tuna is possibly the ultimate convenience seafood, always at the ready for sandwiches, salads or quick pasta sauces. Smoked fillets are particularly delicious. This Mediterranean-inspired salad is simple yet substantial, perfect for a summer lunch.

100 g (3½ oz/1 small bunch) rocket (arugula)
1 small red pepper (capsicum), cut into thin batons
1 small red onion, finely sliced
310 g (11 oz) tinned cannellini beans, drained and rinsed
125 g (4½ oz) cherry tomatoes, cut into halves
2 tablespoons capers, rinsed and squeezed dry
250 g (9 oz) tinned smoked tuna slices in oil, drained
bread to serve

Basil dressing
1 tablespoon lemon juice
1 tablespoon white wine vinegar
60 ml (2 fl oz/¼ cup) extra virgin olive oil
1 garlic clove, crushed
2 tablespoons chopped basil
½ teaspoon sugar

Fish substitution — fresh tuna, seared on both sides and sliced, or tinned salmon

1. Trim any long stems from the rocket, rinse, pat dry and divide among 4 serving plates.

2. Lightly toss the pepper in a large bowl with the onion, beans, tomatoes and capers. Spoon some of this mixture onto the rocket on each plate, then scatter some tuna over each.

3. To make the dressing, thoroughly whisk all the ingredients in a bowl with 1 tablespoon water, ¼ teaspoon salt and freshly ground black pepper to taste. Drizzle over the salad and serve immediately with bread.

Slice the pepper into thin batons

Whisk together all the ingredients for the basil dressing

30 mins

Moules marinières

SERVES 6 * **PREPARATION TIME: 15 MINUTES** * **COOKING TIME: 15 MINUTES**

'A la mariniere' is a French term denoting a dish in which seafood, especially mussels, is cooked in white wine, usually with onions or shallots. The following is a quick and classic way to prepare mussels. Serve them with bread to sop up the delicious juices.

10 g low-fat spread
1 large onion, chopped
½ celery stalk, chopped
2 garlic cloves, crushed
400 ml (14 fl oz) white wine
1 bay leaf
2 sprigs thyme
2 kg (4 lb 8 oz) mussels, cleaned
220 ml (7½ fl oz) light
   evaporated milk
2 tablespoons chopped flat-leaf
   (Italian) parsley
crusty bread to serve

1. Melt the butter in a large saucepan over medium heat. Add the onion, celery and garlic and cook, stirring occasionally, for about 5 minutes, or until the onion is softened but not browned.

2. Add the wine, bay leaf and thyme to the saucepan and bring to the boil. Add the mussels, cover the pan tightly and simmer over low heat for 2–3 minutes, shaking the pan occasionally. Using tongs or a slotted spoon, lift out the mussels as they open and put them into a warm dish. Discard any mussels that haven't opened after 3 minutes.

3. Strain the cooking liquid through a muslin-lined fine sieve into a clean saucepan to remove any grit or sand. Bring the liquid to the boil and boil for 2 minutes. Add the evaporated milk and reheat without boiling. Season well. Serve the mussels in individual bowls with the liquid poured over. Sprinkle with the parsley and serve with bread.

As the mussels open, remove them and place in a warmed dish

Strain the liquid through a sieve lined with muslin into a clean pan

Vietnamese rice paper rolls

SERVES 4–6 ∗ **PREPARATION TIME: 20 MINUTES** ∗ **COOKING TIME: NIL**

Although this recipe may sound fiddly, once you've got the hang of making the rolls — which won't take long at all — you'll find this recipe super easy and quick. The rice paper rolls are very light and fresh tasting, and make a great light lunch or starter.

100 g (3½ oz) vermicelli
20–25 rice paper wrappers, about
   16 cm (6¼ inches) in diameter
40 mint leaves
20 large cooked prawns (shrimp),
   cut in half horizontally
10 garlic chives, halved

Dipping sauce
2 tablespoons satay sauce
60 ml (2 fl oz/¼ cup) hoisin sauce
1 red chilli, finely chopped
1 tablespoon chopped roasted
   unsalted peanuts
1 tablespoon lemon juice

1. Soak the vermicelli for 5 minutes in enough hot water to cover. Drain well and use scissors to roughly chop the noodles into shorter lengths.

2. Using a pastry brush, brush both sides of each rice paper wrapper with water. Leave for about 2 minutes, or until the wrappers become soft and pliable. Stack the wrappers on top of each other, sprinkling each lightly with water to prevent them sticking together and drying out. Be careful, as the wrappers tear easily when softened.

3. Put one softened wrapper on a work surface and spoon about 1 tablespoon of the noodles along the bottom third of the wrapper, leaving enough space at the sides to fold the wrapper over. Top with two mint leaves, two prawn halves and half a garlic chive. Fold in the sides towards each other and firmly roll up the wrapper, allowing the garlic chive to point out of one side. Repeat with the remaining wrappers and ingredients and put the rolls, seam side down, on a serving plate.

4. To make the dipping sauce, combine the satay sauce, hoisin sauce, red chilli, peanuts and lemon juice in a small bowl and mix thoroughly. Serve with the rolls.

Brush both sides of each rice paper wrapper with water

Roll up the rice paper wrapper to firmly enclose the filling

25 mins

Fish kebabs with lemon and herb yoghurt

SERVES 4 ⁎ **PREPARATION TIME: 15 MINUTES + MARINATING TIME**
COOKING TIME: 10 MINUTES

Use any firm, meaty fish fillets, such as tuna, flake, swordfish, kingfish or barramundi, for this quick and easy recipe with Mediterranean flavours. If you are using bamboo skewers, soak them in cold water beforehand to ensure that they will not burn.

800 g (1 lb 12 oz) skinned firm fish
   fillets, cut into 3 cm (1¼ inch)
   chunks
80 ml (2½ fl oz/⅓ cup) lemon juice
80 ml (2½ fl oz/⅓ cup) olive oil
3 bay leaves
16 whole cherry tomatoes, or 2
   firm tomatoes, cut into 8 wedges
2 small red onions, cut into
   8 wedges
2 small red or orange peppers
   (capsicums), seeded and cut into
   8 chunks

Lemon and herb yoghurt
200 g (7 oz/heaped ¾ cup) low-fat
   Greek-style yoghurt
3 teaspoons lemon juice
a pinch paprika
1 tablespoon finely chopped mint
1 tablespoon finely chopped
   flat-leaf (Italian) parsley

Couscous
400 g (14 oz) instant couscous
400 ml (14 fl oz) fish or vegetable
   stock, brought to the boil
1 tablespoon olive oil

1. Put the fish chunks in a non-metallic bowl with the lemon juice, olive oil and bay leaves. Toss to mix, cover and leave to marinate for about 30 minutes in the refrigerator.

2. To make the lemon and herb yoghurt, put all the ingredients in a small bowl and whisk together. Refrigerate until needed.

3. On each of 8 metal skewers, or bamboo skewers that have been soaked for 30 minutes, thread 3 or 4 chunks of fish, 1 cherry tomato, 2 pieces of onion and 2 pieces of pepper, alternating between the fish and the various vegetables as you go.

4. Preheat a barbecue flatplate or griddle pan to high. Brush the kebabs lightly with oil, then cook for 8–10 minutes. Baste with the remaining marinade as they cook, and turn every now and then. When ready, the fish should be firm and opaque and the vegetables slightly charred.

5. Meanwhile, put the couscous into a heatproof bowl, add the stock and oil, cover tightly and leave to sit for 5 minutes or according to the manufacturer's directions. Fluff the grains with a fork. Serve the kebabs on a mound of couscous, accompanied by the yoghurt dressing.

Seed the pepper and chop it into chunks

Toss together the fish, lemon juice, olive oil and bay leaves

Lamb kebabs

SERVES 4 * **PREPARATION TIME: 10 MINUTES** * **COOKING TIME: 20 MINUTES**

Widely sold as street food with Moroccan bread, these spicy lamb kebabs are also often served as a little dish. The meat is cut into small cubes and marinated before being threaded onto bamboo or metal skewers and grilled.

750 g (1 lb 10 oz) lamb loin fillet
1 onion, grated
1 teaspoon paprika
1 teaspoon ground cumin
2 tablespoons finely chopped
    flat-leaf (Italian) parsley
1-2 tablespoons olive oil

Harissa and tomato sauce
2 tomatoes
½ onion, grated to give
    2 tablespoons
1 tablespoon olive oil
1 teaspoon harissa, or to taste
    (or ¼ teaspoon cayenne pepper)
½ teaspoon sugar

1. Cut the meat into 3 cm (1¼ in) cubes and put it in a bowl. Add the onion, paprika, cumin, parsley, olive oil and a generous grind of black pepper. Toss well to coat, then cover and marinate in the refrigerator for at least 2 hours.

2. To make the harissa and tomato sauce, halve the tomatoes horizontally and squeeze out the seeds. Coarsely grate the tomatoes into a bowl down to the skin, discarding the skin. In a saucepan, cook the onion in the olive oil for 2 minutes, stir in the harissa or cayenne pepper, and add the grated tomatoes, sugar and ½ teaspoon salt. Cover and simmer for 10 minutes, then remove the lid and simmer for a further 3-4 minutes, or until the sauce reaches a thick, pouring consistency. Transfer to a bowl.

3. Thread the lamb cubes onto the skewers, leaving a little space between the meat cubes. Heat the barbecue grill to high and cook for 5–6 minutes, turning and brushing with the marinade. Alternatively, cook in a griddle pan or under the grill (broiler).

4. Serve the kebabs with the sauce; alternatively, omit the sauce and serve the kebabs with separate small dishes of ground cumin and salt, to be added according to individual taste.

Use a sharp knife to cut the lamb into large cubes.

Thread the marinated lamb cubes onto skewers.

mains

The recipes in this chapter have been chosen to demonstrate how easily low-fat cooking can become a part of everyday life and how eating healthily doesn't mean you have to compromise on taste. The recipes also show how seafood, vegetables and lean meats are at the heart of a healthy low-fat diet. This selection of recipes can all be cooked in 30 minutes or less and are sourced from all corners of globe, providing fabulous flavour combinations and diversity.

Few other foods offer such an array of shape, size, colour and texture than seafood. As awareness has grown of the importance of seafood in a healthy diet, the quality and range available to us has improved. Cooking with seafood is also a great way to discover different cuisines and new flavour combinations, and to learn new cooking techniques. For a hearty, healthy pasta try the spaghetti alle vongole, which uses clams, or try lightly pan-frying sesame tuna steaks and serving with nori rice.

There is no cuisine that does not rest on a foundation of vegetables. While many of us think of protein as the main event and vegetables as something to go on the side, this is a recent development, allowed only by intensive farming and supermarket convenience. For some scrumptious vegetable main courses that look and taste delicious, try the tagine of fennel, red onions and baby carrots with couscous, the classic French ratatouille or the Indian-inspired celeriac and carrot dahl with naan.

Lean meats might cost you more but they save you time in cooking and, more importantly, provide healthy protein without the saturated fat of cheaper cuts. The recipes that follow reveal the different cuts and meats available and the range of ways in which they can be cooked. Try the the warm salad of watercress, citrus and spring lamb which involves quickly pan-frying lamb fillets, or simply marinate chicken tenderloins and griddle them with asparagus.

The key to creating a meal that is light and yet still satisfying is to go small on quantity but big on flavour. The perfect low-fat dish is one that fills you up without weighing you down. Seafood and lean meats served with piles of delectable vegetables and salads work brilliantly whether you're hosting a dinner party or just sitting down to a quiet meal with the family.

Phad thai

SERVES 4 ＊ **PREPARATION TIME: 15 MINUTES** ＊ **COOKING TIME: 5 MINUTES**

Phad thai is one of Thailand's favourite street foods and is popular in Thai restaurants the world over. This tasty noodle dish is full of flavour, fresh ingredients and is so simple to prepare.

10 or 20 raw tiger prawns or small prawns, peeled and deveined

200 g (7 oz) medium-thickness dried rice noodles

1 tablespoon dried shrimp

1-2 tablespoons vegetable oil

2 garlic cloves, crushed

1 small red chilli, finely chopped

2 tablespoons grated palm sugar (jaggery) or soft brown sugar

3 tablespoons lemon juice

2 tablespoons fish sauce

4 tablespoons peanuts, toasted and roughly chopped

3 spring onions (scallions), sliced on the diagonal

90 g (3¼ oz/1 cup) bean sprouts, tails trimmed

3 tablespoons coriander (cilantro) leaves

lemon wedges to serve

Note: To make this dish vegetarian, omit the prawns, shrimp paste and fish sauce. Replace the prawns with 250 g (9 oz) tofu puffs, adding them to the wok at the same time as the garlic and chilli. Replace the fish sauce with 1 tablespoon of soy sauce.

1. If using tiger prawns, chop each one into three or four pieces, depending on size. Put the rice noodles in a bowl and cover with boiling water. Put the dried shrimp in a cup and cover with boiling water. Leave both to soak for 10 minutes, then drain. Make sure you have all the other ingredients at the ready before you start cooking.

2. Heat the oil in a wok over high heat until smoking. Add the beaten egg and cook for 30 seconds, then stir to break into small pieces. Add the garlic, chilli and prawns and cook for 15 seconds, stirring all the time.

3. Add the sugar, lemon juice and fish sauce and cook for 15 seconds, stirring and tossing in the wok. Tip in the noodles, dried shrimp and 3 tablespoons of the peanuts. Toss together in the wok to heat through before adding the spring onion and bean sprouts. Cook for a further 30 seconds, then tip onto a serving plate and scatter the coriander and remaining peanuts over the top. Serve immediately with the lemon wedges.

Griddled asparagus and chicken

SERVES 4 ∗ **PREPARATION TIME: 10 MINUTES + MARINATING TIME**
COOKING TIME: 8 MINUTES

Asparagus cooks beautifully on the griddle pan. Its flavour is intensified and it tends to stay crisp and bright. Many believe that the biggest benefit is in the timing — where a matter of seconds can be critical when steaming or boiling, grilling offers a lot more leeway.

Dressing
80 ml (2½ fl oz/⅓ cup)
   groundnut oil
2 tablespoons reduced fat
   coconut milk
2 teaspoons lime juice
1 teaspoon grated kaffir lime
   (makrut) zest
2 garlic cloves, crushed
½ teaspoon finely chopped mint

6 medium (about 225 g/8 oz)
   chicken tenderloins
16 asparagus spears, trimmed
oil spray for cooking
1 handful small mint leaves
½ long green chilli, seeded and
   finely shredded

1. To make the dressing, put half the oil, the coconut milk, lime juice, lime zest and garlic in a small bowl and season with a little salt and plenty of freshly ground black pepper. Mix well.

2. Trim the white sinew from the thick end of the chicken tenderloins and halve them lengthways. Put the chicken and asparagus spears in a shallow non-metallic dish. Pour in half the dressing and toss to coat. Set aside to marinate for 30 minutes. Add the remaining oil and the mint to the other half of the dressing.

3. Spray a hot barbecue plate or griddle pan with oil. Remove the asparagus and chicken from the marinade, drain and cook for 7–8 minutes, or until browned and cooked through, turning the asparagus often and the chicken once. Discard the marinade.

4. Transfer the asparagus and chicken to a bowl, add the mint leaves and chilli and toss lightly. Pile in the centre of 4 plates and drizzle with the dressing. Serve warm or at room temperature.

Marinate the chicken strips and the asparagus in the dressing

Griddle until browned and cooked through

Warm salad of watercress, citrus and spring lamb

SERVES 4 ✳ **PREPARATION TIME: 15 MINUTES** ✳ **COOKING TIME: 4 MINUTES**

This salad is spring on a plate: the zing of citrus combines with the peppery, mustardy taste of raw watercress leaves to complement seared lamb. For the tenderest results, try spring lamb (3–10 months old) or milk-fed lamb (generally under 8 weeks of age).

Dressing
1 tablespoon red wine vinegar
1 garlic clove, crushed
½ teaspoon honey
2 teaspoons walnut oil
1½ tablespoons olive oil

300 g (10½ oz) lamb fillets
olive oil spray for pan-frying
2 oranges
1 small pink grapefruit
3 large handfuls watercress, picked over
½ small red onion, finely sliced

1. To make the dressing, put all the ingredients in a small bowl, season with salt and freshly ground black pepper and whisk to combine.

2. Cut the lamb fillets in half and season with freshly ground black pepper. Lightly spray the olive oil in a frying pan over high heat and cook the lamb for 3–4 minutes, or until browned, turning once or twice. Season with salt and remove from the heat.

3. Peel the oranges and grapefruit, removing all the white pith. Holding them over a bowl to catch the juice, segment them by using a small, sharp knife to cut between the membranes. Put the segments in the bowl with the juices.

4. Cut the lamb on the diagonal into 2.5 cm (1 inch) thick slices and add to the bowl, along with the watercress and red onion. Pour the dressing over the salad and lightly toss to coat.

watercress

Too often, watercress is seen as nothing more than a garnish. While its dainty form and deep, luscious colour are certainly decorative, the powerful little leaves of this aquatic plant have a versatility and impact that belie their fragile appearance. Using watercress is a simple way to bring a complex, peppery edge to a dish without disturbing the delicate balance of flavours. Like most dark green, leafy vegetables, watercress is an excellent source of iron. Fresh is always best, so try growing your own. As with any type of cress, it must be washed thoroughly before use. Buy dark leaves with no yellowing and use quickly. To store, stand stems in a bowl of water, cover with a plastic bag and refrigerate.

30 mins

Spaghetti alle vongole

SERVES 4 * PREPARATION TIME: 15 MINUTES * COOKING TIME: 15 MINUTES

Vongole is simply the Italian word for clam. Clams vary in size and shape from region to region; ask your fishmonger for the best local variety. Even if they are sold as cleaned, it's worth giving them an extra clean yourself.

1 tablespoon olive oil
3 garlic cloves, crushed
2 pinches chilli flakes
125 ml (4 fl oz/½ cup) dry
  white wine
400 g (14 oz) tinned chopped
  tomatoes
3 tablespoons finely chopped
  flat-leaf (Italian) parsley
1 kg (2 lb 4 oz) clams, cleaned
400 g (14 oz) dried spaghetti
  or linguine
½ teaspoon grated lemon zest
lemon halves to serve

Shellfish substitution — small mussels

1. Heat the oil in a large, deep frying pan. Add the garlic and chilli and cook over low heat for 30 seconds. Add the white wine, tomatoes and 1 teaspoon of the parsley. Increase the heat and boil, stirring occasionally, for 8–10 minutes, or until the liquid is reduced by half.

2. Add the clams to the pan and cover with a lid. Increase the heat and cook for 3–5 minutes, or until the clams have opened, shaking the pan often. Remove the clams from the pan, discarding any that have not opened. Stir in the remaining parsley and season. Boil the sauce for 3–4 minutes until it is thick. Set half the clams aside and extract the meat from the rest.

3. Cook the pasta in a large saucepan of boiling salted water until al dente. Drain and stir through the sauce. Add the lemon zest, reserved clams and clam meat and toss well. Serve with the lemon halves.

pasta

Pasta is one of the world's great foods. Cheap, durable in its dried form and endlessly versatile, it has been adopted by cooks the world over. The types and shapes of pasta are many: spirals, long strands or ribbons, large shells, and dozens more. Long, thin pastas, which include spaghetti and linguine, are excellent for serving with simple sauces that will stick to their lengths without falling off, or with seafood such as clams, as the clams can be easily picked out and the flesh removed from the shells. Spaghetti alle vongole is a classic seafood and pasta combination; although, in fact, most shellfish is delicious with pasta.

30 mins

Tagine of fennel, red onions and baby carrots with couscous

SERVES 4 * **PREPARATION TIME: 10 MINUTES** * **COOKING TIME: 20 MINUTES**

In North Africa, and particularly in Morocco, a tagine is an earthenware dish with a conical lid in which stews are simmered. The stews, also called tagines, are characterized by having both savoury and sweet flavours. They are served with couscous, as here, or rice.

3 baby fennel bulbs
6 small (about 80 g/2¾ oz each) red onions
8 baby carrots
375 ml (13 fl oz/1½ cups) chicken stock
1 teaspoon ground ginger
1 scant teaspoon ground cumin
½ teaspoon ground cinnamon
1½ tablespoons honey
5 garlic cloves
1 cinnamon stick
2 tablespoons raisins
1 small handful mint

Saffron couscous
a small pinch saffron threads
625 ml (22 fl oz/2½ cups) chicken stock or water
375 g (13 oz/2 cups) instant couscous
1 tablespoon olive oil

1. Trim the tops off the fennel, leaving 2–3 cm (¾–1¼ inches) of stalks remaining, and discard the tough outer leaves. Halve the fennel lengthways. Peel the onions, leaving the ends intact. Trim the carrots, leaving 1–2 cm (½–¾ inch) of stalks remaining. Scrub the carrots. Place vegetables in a microwave-safe dish with a little water, cover and cook on high for 4-5 minutes.

2. Put the stock in a flameproof casserole dish and add the fennel, onions, carrots, ground ginger, cumin, cinnamon, honey, garlic and cinnamon stick. Bring to the boil, then add the currants. Cover and simmer over low heat for 15 minutes, or until the vegetables are soft. Toss the mint leaves through the tagine.

3. Meanwhile, to make the saffron couscous, soak the saffron in 2 tablespoons hot water for 10 minutes. Bring the stock to the boil in a medium saucepan. Stir in the couscous and saffron with its soaking liquid. Cover and cook for 3 minutes. Remove from the heat and set aside for 5 minutes. Add the olive oil and toss with a fork to loosen the grains. Serve with the vegetables.

Halve the trimmed fennel bulbs lengthways

Add the vegetables and cinnamon stick to the pot

Sesame tuna steaks with nori rice

SERVES 4 ∗ **PREPARATION TIME: 10 MINUTES** ∗ **COOKING TIME: 20 MINUTES**

Tuna, so tasty when served as sashimi or as a sushi topping, is also very delicious cooked. These steaks, coated with crunchy sesame seeds, are sauteed only until the crust is golden, bringing out the nutty aroma while leaving the tuna rare.

4 x 200 g (7 oz) tuna steaks
115 g (4 oz/¾ cup) sesame seeds
200 g (7 oz/1 cup) medium-grain rice
2½ tablespoons rice wine vinegar
1 tablespoon mirin
1 teaspoon sugar
1 nori sheet, finely shredded
oil spray for pan-frying
125 g (4½ oz/½ cup) light mayonnaise
2 teaspoons wasabi paste
pickled ginger to serve, optional

1. Coat the tuna steaks in the sesame seeds, pressing down to coat well. Refrigerate until needed.

2. Wash the rice until the water runs clear, then put in a saucepan with 500 ml (17 fl oz/2 cups) water. Bring to the boil, then reduce the heat to very low and cook, covered, for 10–12 minutes. Turn off the heat and leave, covered, for 5 minutes. While hot, pour on the combined rice wine vinegar, mirin, sugar and ¼ teaspoon salt. Stir with a fork to separate the grains, then fold in the shredded nori. Keep warm.

3. Lightly spray the oil in a large frying pan, add the tuna steaks and cook for 1–2 minutes on each side, or until the sesame seeds are crisp and golden. The tuna should still be a little pink in the middle. Drain on paper towels.

4. Spoon the rice into four lightly greased 125 ml (4 fl oz/½ cup) ramekins or cups, pressing down lightly, then invert onto each plate and remove the ramekins. Combine the mayonnaise and wasabi in a small bowl. Serve the tuna with the nori rice and with some wasabi mayonnaise on the side. Garnish with pickled ginger, if desired.

Press down on the sesame seeds so they adhere to the tuna

Fry the sesame-coated tuna until the seeds are golden

Three ways with scallops

Scallops are found in all seas. The many species can all be cooked in the same ways, or eaten raw. All have fan-shaped shells, white meat and edible orange-red roe. If bought opened but still on the half-shell, they will need to be rinsed, as they can be sandy. If bought whole, they will need to be scrubbed. Discard any that are open but do not close quickly when sharply tapped. Once cooked, the shells should open up; discard any that remain closed.

Scallop ceviche

SERVES 4 ∗ **PREPARATION TIME: 15 MINUTES** ∗ **COOKING TIME: NIL**

Clean 16 scallops in their closed shells by scrubbing under running water. One by one, hold the scallop in a tea towel and, with a sharp knife or an oyster knife, carefully prise open the shell. Lift off the top shell and loosen the scallop from the shell. Pull off and discard the scallop's outer grey fringe and outer membrane. Retain the shells. In a non-metallic bowl, mix together 1 teaspoon finely grated lime zest, 60 ml (2 fl oz/¼ cup) lime juice, 2 chopped garlic cloves, 2 seeded and chopped red chillies, 1 tablespoon chopped coriander (cilantro) leaves and 1 tablespoon olive oil. Season with salt and freshly ground black pepper. Put the scallops in the dressing and stir to coat. Cover with plastic wrap and refrigerate for 2 hours; the acid in the lime juice will 'cold-cook' the scallop flesh. To serve, slide each scallop back onto a half shell and spoon a little of the lime dressing over it. Top each scallop with a whole coriander leaf. Serve cold. For an attractive presentation, the scallops in their half shells can be placed on a bed of rock salt or crushed ice on a large platter.

Scallops in black bean sauce

SERVES 4 ∗ **PREPARATION TIME: 10 MINUTES** ∗ **COOKING TIME: 5 MINUTES**

Clean 24 scallops in their closed shells by scrubbing under running water. Heat 1 tablespoon oil in a wok and, when hot, add the scallops. Cook for 2 minutes, or until just firm. (Do not overcook, or they will be tough and rubbery.) Transfer to a plate. Mix together 1 tablespoon soy sauce, 2 tablespoons Chinese rice wine, 1 teaspoon sugar and 1 tablespoon water and set aside. Add another 1 tablespoon oil to the wok and heat until it is beginning to smoke. Add 1 finely chopped garlic clove, 1 finely chopped spring onion (scallion) and ½ teaspoon finely grated fresh ginger. Cook for 30 seconds. Add 1 tablespoon rinsed and drained salted fermented black beans and the reserved soy sauce mixture and bring to the boil. Return the scallops to the sauce with 1 teaspoon roasted sesame oil and allow to simmer for about 30 seconds. Serve immediately with rice and steamed Asian greens.

Shellfish substitution — prawns (shrimp), crayfish or lobster, baby squid

Barbecued asian-style scallops

SERVES 2 ∗ **PREPARATION TIME: 10 MINUTES** ∗ **COOKING TIME: 5 MINUTES**

Put 300 g (10½ oz) scallop meat in a shallow non-metallic bowl. In a separate bowl, combine 80 ml (2½ fl oz/⅓ cup) sweet chilli sauce, 1 teaspoon fish sauce, 2 teaspoons lime juice and 1 teaspoon peanut oil. Pour the mixture over the scallop meat and mix gently to coat. Allow to marinate for 1 hour. Drain the seafood well and reserve the marinade. Preheat a griddle pan to high, add 1 tablespoon peanut oil and heat. Cook the scallops for 3–5 minutes, or until tender. Drizzle with a little of the leftover marinade during cooking. Serve on a bed of steamed rice with wedges of lime.

Boeuf à la ficelle

SERVES 4 ∗ **PREPARATION TIME: 10 MINUTES** ∗ **COOKING TIME: 20 MINUTES**

Beef fillet — a lean, tender cut — is normally grilled, pan-fried or roasted. In this classic preparation it is poached in beef stock. The name translates as 'beef on a string', in reference to the kitchen string used to tie the beef, lower it into the stock then raise it when cooked.

800 g (1 lb 12 oz) centre-cut
   beef fillet
900 ml (31 fl oz) beef stock
1 swede (rutabaga), cut into batons
1 carrot, cut into batons
1 celery stalk, cut into batons
2 potatoes, cut into chunks
¼ cabbage, chopped
4 spring onions (scallions),
   trimmed into long lengths
1 bay leaf
2 thyme sprigs
2 flat-leaf (Italian) parsley sprigs

1. Trim the beef of any fat and sinew and cut into four even pieces. Tie each piece of beef around its circumference with kitchen string so it keeps its compact shape. Leave a long length of string attached, to lower the beef in and out of the stock.

2. Put the stock in a saucepan, bring to the boil and add the vegetables and herbs. Cook over medium heat for about 8 minutes, or until the vegetables are tender. Lift out the vegetables with a slotted spoon and keep warm. Discard the herbs and skim the stock of any foam that floats to the surface.

3. Season the beef with salt, then lower into the simmering stock, keeping the strings tied around the saucepan handle or a wooden spoon balanced over the pan. Cook for about 6 minutes for rare, or 10 minutes for medium–rare, depending on your taste.

4. Place each piece of beef in a large shallow bowl and loop the end of the string onto the rim of the bowl. Add the cooked vegetables and ladle some of the cooking broth over the top to serve.

swedes

Swedes have an earthy sweetness that is quite delicious and one that is perfectly complementary to the deep, savoury flavours of this poached beef dish. A winter vegetable, they are the result of a seventeenth century cross between the turnip and the cabbage. Choose swedes that are heavy for their size. Swedes are a long-keeping vegetable and are often sold with a wax coating — in any case they need peeling before using and, if the layer under the skin is fibrous, pare this away too.

30 mins

Ratatouille

SERVES 4 * **PREPARATION TIME: 10 MINUTES** * **COOKING TIME: 20 MINUTES**

Be sure to make ratatouille in the summer months, when basil, courgette (zucchini) and tomatoes are at their best. There are many ways to prepare this dish. Here, the vegetables are sautéed separately before being simmered together — this may seem laborious but it is worth it.

800 g (1 lb 12 oz) cans peeled
   tomatoes
1 tablespoon olive oil
1 large onion, diced
1 red pepper (capsicum), diced
1 yellow pepper (capsicum), diced
1 aubergine (eggplant), diced
2 courgettes (zucchini), diced
1 teaspoon tomato purée (paste)
½ teaspoon sugar
1 bay leaf
3 thyme sprigs
2 basil sprigs
1 garlic clove, crushed
1 tablespoon chopped flat-leaf
   (Italian) parsley

1. Heat the oil in a frying pan. Add the onion and cook over low heat for 2-3 minutes. Add the peppers and cook, stirring, for 3-4 minutes. Remove from the pan and set aside.

2. Fry the aubergine and courgettes until lightly browned all over. Return the onion and peppers to the pan. Add the tomato paste, tomatoes, sugar, bay leaf, thyme and basil. Stir well, cover and cook for 10–15 minutes. Remove the bay leaf, thyme and basil.

3. Mix together the garlic and parsley and add to the ratatouille at the last minute. Stir and serve.

Before dicing peppers, remove ribs, membranes and seeds.

Sauté the vegetables separately as cooking times vary.

30 mins

Steamed sake chicken

SERVES 4 ∗ **PREPARATION TIME: 10 MINUTES + MARINATING TIME**
COOKING TIME: 20 MINUTES

Sake, Japan's beloved rice brew, can be a wonderful marinade base. Enhanced with a variety of Asian seasonings, it gives these steamed chicken breasts a particularly inviting tenderness and flavour.

500 g (1 lb 2 oz) skinless
   chicken breasts
80 ml (2½ fl oz/⅓ cup) sake
2 tablespoons lemon juice
4 cm (1½ in) piece fresh ginger,
   thinly sliced
2 tablespoons shoyu (Japanese soy
   sauce)
1 tablespoon mirin
1 teaspoon sesame oil
1 spring onion (scallion), sliced
   on the diagonal, plus extra
   to garnish
½ small red pepper (capsicum),
   skin removed, flesh cut into thin
   3 cm (1¼ in) long strips

1. Place the chicken in a shallow dish, then pour over the combined sake, lemon juice, ginger and 1 teaspoon salt. Cover and marinate in the refrigerator for 30 minutes.

2. Combine the shoyu, mirin, sesame oil and spring onion in a small bowl and set aside.

3. Line a steamer with baking paper. Arrange the chicken, in the steamer. Fill a saucepan with 500 ml (17 fl oz/2 cups) water and sit the steamer over the top. Cover and cook over simmering water for 20 minutes, or until cooked.

4. Cut the chicken into bite-sized pieces, put into a serving bowl and drizzle with the shoyu mixture. Garnish with the pepper strips and extra spring onion. Serve with rice.

sake

In ancient times, sake was brewed for the gods and shamans alone. Today this popular alcoholic beverage, also called nihonshu, is an ideal accompaniment to many Japanese dishes. Its alcohol content ranges from 16–19 per cent, and it is produced in amazing variety by some 2000 breweries. Customarily served warm in the winter, heating helps to improve the taste of lower quality sake. The best, however, are most delicious when served at room temperature or chilled. Sake is often explained as 'rice wine' but because it is brewed it is not a true wine. In certain dishes, however, it is used as a seasoning, just as wine is used in French cooking.

28 mins

Udon noodle soup

SERVES 4 ∗ **PREPARATION TIME: 10 MINUTES** ∗ **COOKING TIME: 18 MINUTES**

For those who love the flavour and texture of udon noodles, this quick and easy broth is made with instant dashi granules. The noodles must not be overcooked, as they should retain some substance — what the Japanese call koshi.

400 g (14 oz) dried udon noodles

3 teaspoons dashi granules

2 leeks, white and pale green parts, washed well and cut into very thin slices

200 g (7 oz) pork loin, cut into thin strips

125 ml (4 fl oz/½ cup) shoyu (Japanese soy sauce)

2 tablespoons mirin

3 spring onions (scallions), 2 cut into 4 cm (1½ in) lengths, 1 finely chopped

shichimi togarashi (seven-spice mix) to serve

Note: Shichimi togarashi is a Japanese mixed chilli pepper, and is available from Japanese grocers. A little chilli powder may be used in place of shichimi togarashi.

1. Cook the noodles in a large saucepan of rapidly boiling water for 5 minutes, or until tender. Drain and cover to keep warm.

2. Combine 1 litre (35 fl oz/4 cups) water and the dashi granules in a large pan and bring to the boil. Add the leeks, then reduce the heat and simmer for 5 minutes. Add the pork, shoyu, mirin and lengths of spring onion and simmer for 2 minutes, or until the pork is cooked.

3. Divide the noodles among four serving bowls and ladle the soup over the top. Garnish with the chopped spring onion and sprinkle the shichimi togarashi over the top.

shichimi togarashi

Shichimi togarashi, meaning 'seven-flavour hot red pepper', is a blend of togarashi pepper with at least six other spices. The ingredients and their proportions vary by region, maker and individual preferences. Typically the mix can contain any of the following: black or white sesame seeds, ground sansho pods, poppy seeds, mustard, hemp seeds, rape seeds, nori flakes, and sometimes chinpi, the dried peel of citron, bitter orange or tangerine. Although available in any supermarket in Japan, it is a favourite souvenir item among Japanese, purchased at spice shops while visiting old Kyoto or other famous tourist sites. The spice mix is sprinkled on soups, noodles and meat dishes.

Steamed snapper with Asian flavours

SERVES 2 ✳ **PREPARATION TIME: 10 MINUTES** ✳ **COOKING TIME: 20 MINUTES**

There are various species of fish known as snappers in Caribbean, Pacific and Asian waters. Most make very fine eating. As they age, some species develop a distinctive bulge above the eyes. Lemon grass, coriander (cilantro) and ginger add a piquant Asian touch to this dish.

1 whole snapper, weighing about 800 g (1 lb 12 oz), scaled, fins removed and gutted
3 stems lemon grass
a handful coriander (cilantro) leaves
3 cm (1¼ inch) piece fresh ginger, peeled and cut into thin matchsticks
1 large garlic clove, peeled and cut into thin slivers
2 tablespoons soy sauce
1 tablespoon oil
1 tablespoon fish sauce
1 small red chilli, seeded and finely diced
stir-fried Asian greens to serve

Fish substitution — sea bass

1. Score the fish with diagonal cuts on both sides. Cut each lemon grass stem into three and lightly squash each piece with the end of the handle of a large knife. Put half of the lemon grass in the middle of a large piece of foil and lay the fish on top. Put the remaining lemon grass and half the coriander inside the cavity of the fish.

2. Mix the ginger, garlic, soy sauce, oil, fish sauce and chilli together in a bowl. Drizzle the mixture over the fish and scatter the remaining coriander leaves over.

3. Enclose the fish in the foil and place in a bamboo or metal steamer over a large saucepan of simmering water. Steam for 20-25 minutes, or until the flesh of the fish is opaque and white. Transfer the foil package to a large serving plate and open at the table. Serve the fish with stir-fried Asian greens.

coriander

Fresh coriander (also known as cilantro) is thought to be the world's most commonly used herb. Every part can be used: roots, stems, leaves and seeds. Different cuisines favour different parts: the seeds figure highly in European cooking, the roots are pounded for use in Thai curry pastes and the fresh leaves are used liberally in Southeast Asian and Latin American cooking. From India to Indonesia, the seeds are a vital part of curry pastes and spice mixes. In most Asian cooking, coriander leaves and roots are a key component in fish and shellfish dishes, due to the herb's aromatic flavour and natural affinity with such ingredients as ginger, chillies, lemon grass and lime juice.

Three ways with spinach

Fresh, leafy spinach has a certain dark and loamy essence. It's almost as though you can taste the iron that makes it so good for you. It's easy to bring out the best in spinach when it's simply stir-fried with smoked tofu and Asian greens. Baked with eggs, spring onions and provolone, spinach becomes a soft swirl of nourishing wholesomeness. Tossed through hot spaghetti with pine nuts and pancetta, the gently wilted leaves brings a ferrous tang to the dish.

Stir-fried spinach with tofu and Asian greens

SERVES 4 ✳ **PREPARATION TIME: 10 MINUTES** ✳ **COOKING TIME: 5 MINUTES**

To make the dressing, put 2 tablespoons each of lime juice and vegetable oil, 1½ tablespoons fish sauce, 1 teaspoon sambal oelek (or chilli paste) and ½ teaspoon light brown sugar in a bowl and whisk well. Cut 200 g (7 oz) smoked tofu or firm tofu into 1.5–2 cm (5/8–¾ inch) cubes. Trim 400 g (14 oz/1 bunch) choy sum (or other Asian greens) and cut it into 7–8 cm (2¾–3¼ inch) lengths. Heat 1 tablespoon oil in a large wok over medium heat and gently stir-fry the tofu for 2–3 minutes, or until golden brown. Add half the dressing and toss to coat. Remove from the wok and set aside. Add the choy sum to the wok and stir-fry for 1 minute. Add 150 g (5½ oz) torn spinach and stir-fry for 1 minute. Return the tofu to the wok, add 2 teaspoons toasted sesame seeds and the remaining dressing and toss lightly. Serve with 1 small handful coriander (cilantro) leaves piled on top.

Baked eggs and spinach

SERVES 4 ✳ **PREPARATION TIME: 10 MINUTES** ✳ **COOKING TIME: 20 MINUTES**

Heat 1 tablespoon olive oil in a frying pan over high heat. Add 80 g (2¾ oz/2 cups) coarsely chopped spinach and 4 thinly sliced spring onions (scallions). Cook, stirring, for 30–40 seconds, or until the spinach has wilted. Season with a pinch of nutmeg and season with salt and pepper. Divide the spinach among 4 lightly greased 150 ml (5 fl oz) ramekins. Crack an egg into each ramekin and sprinkle 1-2 tablespoons grated provolone or gouda cheese (optional) over the top. Transfer the ramekins to a roasting tin half filled with hot water. Bake in a preheated 180°C (350°F/Gas 4) oven for 20-25 minutes, or until the eggs are just set.

Spaghetti with spinach, pine nuts and smoked ham

SERVES 4 ✳ **PREPARATION TIME: 10 MINUTES** ✳ **COOKING TIME: 2 MINUTES**

Cook 350 g (12 oz) spaghetti in a large saucepan of boiling salted water until al dente according to the manufacturer's instructions. Slice 4 thin slices of smoked ham into strips. Heat 1 tablespoon olive oil in a large frying pan over medium heat and stir-fry the ham and 40 g (1½ oz/¼ cup) pine nuts for 1½–2 minutes, or until the ham is crisp and the nuts are golden. Stir in 60 g (2¼ oz/¼ cup) half fat crème fraîche. Drain the pasta and add it to the pan. Add 100 g (3½ oz) spinach, torn into small pieces, and toss well to coat. Serve topped with parmesan shavings (optional).

Laksa lemak

SERVES 4 * **PREPARATION TIME: 10 MINUTES** * **COOKING TIME: 20 MINUTES**

A robustly flavoured soup, laksa is a meal in itself. It features rice noodles, seafood or chicken and various garnishes in a spicy stock. Laksa lemak, the Singaporean version, is rich with coconut milk and is the most popular type.

300 g (10½ oz) straight-to-wok
   rice noodles
50 g (1¾ oz) unsalted macadamias
1 tablespoon oil
400 ml (28 fl oz) tinned reduced fat
   coconut milk
400ml (28 fl oz) tinned light
   evaporated milk
80 ml (2½ fl oz/⅓ cup) lime juice
115 g (4 oz) bean sprouts, trimmed
20 large raw prawns (shrimp),
   peeled and deveined
16 large scallops, cleaned
a handful Vietnamese mint,
   shredded, a few leaves left whole
   to garnish
½ Lebanese (short) cucumber,
   peeled and thinly sliced

Paste
3 red chillies, seeded and chopped
2 stems lemon grass
a small knob fresh ginger, grated
4 red Asian shallots, peeled
3 teaspoons shrimp paste
3 teaspoons ground turmeric

   Fish substitution — cubes of any
   firm-fleshed white fish

   Note: ¼ regular cucumber may
   be used in place of ½ Lebanese
   (short) cucumber.

1. To make the paste, put all the paste ingredients, plus 1 tablespoon water, into a food processor and blend until smooth. Alternatively, finely chop by hand and mix well.

2. Put the nuts in a saucepan and dry-roast over medium heat, shaking the pan, until golden. Transfer to a plate.

3. Heat the oil in the same saucepan, add the prepared paste and cook over medium heat for 2 minutes. Stir in the coconut milk and evaporated milk, then gently simmer for 10 minutes, or until it thickens slightly. Roughly chop the nuts.

4. When the coconut milk mixture is ready, add the lime juice and three-quarters of the bean sprouts to the pan. Season with salt, bring back to a simmer, then add the prawns and scallops and cook for about 5 minutes, or until the prawns have turned pink. Add the shredded mint and the noodles. Mix the whole mint leaves with the chopped nuts and cucumber.

5. Ladle into 4 deep bowls, then sprinkle with the remaining bean sprouts and the mint and cucumber mixture.

30 mins

Trout stuffed with dates

SERVES 4 ❋ **PREPARATION TIME: 10 MINUTES** ❋ **COOKING TIME: 20 MINUTES**

The marriage of dates with fish is a time-honoured practice in Morocco. Traditionally the stuffed fish would be cooked in a tagine, but with domestic ovens now more widely available, it is often oven-baked. The foil wrapping keeps the fish moist.

4 medium trout
140 g (5 oz/¾ cup) chopped dates
50 g (1¾ oz/¼ cup) cooked rice
1 onion, finely chopped
4 tablespoons chopped coriander (cilantro) leaves
¼ teaspoon ground ginger
¼ teaspoon ground cinnamon, plus extra to serve
50 g (1¾ oz/⅓ cup) roughly chopped blanched almonds
40 g (1½ oz) butter, softened

1. Preheat the oven to 180°C (350°F/Gas 4). Rinse the trout under cold running water and pat them dry with paper towels. Season lightly with salt and freshly ground black pepper.

2. Combine the dates, cooked rice, half the onion, the coriander, ginger, cinnamon, almonds and half the butter in a bowl. Season well with salt and freshly ground black pepper.

3. Spoon the stuffing into the fish cavities and place each fish on a well-greased double sheet of foil. Brush the fish with the remaining butter, season with salt and freshly ground black pepper and divide the remaining onion among the four parcels. Wrap the fish neatly and seal the edges of the foil. Place the parcels on a large baking tray and bake for 15–20 minutes, or until cooked to your liking. Serve dusted with ground cinnamon.

30 mins

Celeriac and carrot dahl with naan

SERVES 4 ✳ **PREPARATION TIME: 10 MINUTES** ✳ **COOKING TIME: 20 MINUTES**

To ensure a firm, uniform flesh, choose celeriac that are about the size of a grapefruit. Those with smoother surfaces will be easier to peel. Once peeled and exposed to air, the flesh will discolour, so have a bowl of acidulated water on hand if the cut pieces are not to be used immediately.

1 tablespoon olive oil
1 teaspoon yellow mustard seeds
1 onion, chopped
2 garlic cloves, crushed
1 tablespoon finely grated
  fresh ginger
2 teaspoons cumin seeds
1 tablespoon ground coriander
½ teaspoon ground turmeric
2 teaspoons sambal oelek
820 g (1 lb 13 oz) tinned lentils,
  drained and rinsed
1 medium celeriac, peeled and cut
  into 2 cm (¾ inch) chunks
2 carrots, peeled and cut into
  2 cm (¾ inch) chunks
1 handful mint, coarsely chopped
  if large
naan to serve

Note: Sambal oelek is available in good supermarkets, Asian and Thai grocers. Chilli paste may be used as a substitute for sambal oelek in this recipe.

1. Heat the olive oil in a large non-aluminium saucepan over low heat and add the mustard seeds. When they start to pop, add the onion, garlic and ginger. Fry for 4–5 minutes, stirring often. Add the cumin seeds, ground coriander, turmeric and sambal oelek, increase the heat and fry for 1 minute.

2. Add the celeriac and carrot and stir to coat. Add 750 ml (26 fl oz/3 cups) hot water and bring to the boil. Reduce the heat and simmer for 10-15 minutes or until the vegetables are tender and most of the liquid has been absorbed. Add the lentils and cook for 2 minutes. Season with salt, to taste, stir through the mint and serve with naan.

celeriac

As its name suggests, celeriac is a member of the celery family and has a taste reminiscent of both celery and parsley. This versatile root can be used in a recipe in place of celery, or treated as a vegetable in its own right. The skin is fairly inedible and should be removed before use unless you are planning to bake the root whole. The leaves and stalks are useful for assessing freshness (they should be pert and bright) but are inedible and should be removed before you store the celeriac in the fridge. Celeriac is relatively low in carbohydrates and can be used in place of potato for those who are counting grams of carbohydrate.

Teriyaki chicken

SERVES 4 ✳ **PREPARATION TIME: 10 MINUTES** ✳ **COOKING TIME: 10 MINUTES**

Teriyaki sauce gives chicken an attractive and delicious glaze that proves its literal meaning: 'lustre grilling (broiling)'. It is so simple to make that it seems surprising that the instant bottled sauces would have ever found a market.

60 ml (2 fl oz/¼ cup) shoyu
   (Japanese soy sauce)
2 tablespoons mirin
2 tablespoons sake
1½ tablespoons caster (superfine)
   sugar
oil spray for cooking
4 x 200 g boneless chicken thighs
   (7 oz) with skin, or cutlets with
   the bone removed

1. Combine the shoyu, mirin, sake and sugar in a small bowl and stir until the sugar has dissolved. Set aside.

2. Lightly spray the oil in a large, heavy-based frying pan over medium–high heat. Add the chicken, skin side down, and cook for 4–5 minutes, or until the skin is golden. Turn the chicken over and cook for a further 3–4 minutes, or until golden and almost cooked through. Remove from the pan.

3. Discard any excess fat from the pan, then pour in the shoyu mixture, increase the heat to high and bring to the boil. Cook for 1 minute, or until the liquid has slightly reduced and is glossy. Return the chicken and any juices to the pan and turn to coat well. Remove from the pan and slice on a slight angle into 1.5 cm (⅝ in) wide strips. Holding the chicken thighs in their original shape, transfer to a plate or bowl. Serve with rice and vegetables or a salad.

soy sauce

Soy sauce, shoyu, is so valued in Japanese cuisine that it is usually referred to with the honorific 'o' prefix. Indeed, soy sauce is used as commonly in Japan as salt is used in the West. O-shoyu is made from a fermentation of soya beans, wheat, water and salt. Of the several main varieties, koikuchi shoyu, the regular dark sauce, is most widely used, whereas usukuchi shoyu, a light-coloured sauce, is useful for dishes in which a darker sauce might give an unappealing or 'dirty' appearance. Tamari-joyu, an intense, dark, slightly thicker sauce, usually made without wheat, is the dipping sauce of choice for sashimi. The best quality soy sauces can take up to 2 years to make.

30 mins

Saffron fish balls in tomato sauce

SERVES 4 ✳ **PREPARATION TIME: 10 MINUTES** ✳ **COOKING TIME: 20 MINUTES**

This recipe was devised by Moroccan Jews, who were also the principal gatherers of the saffron crocus when it was introduced from Moorish Spain. It is based on their traditional recipe for fish balls, but with distinctive Moroccan flavours. Any white fish fillets can be used.

500 g (1 lb 2 oz) boneless white fish fillets

1 egg

2 spring onions (scallions), chopped

1 tablespoon chopped flat-leaf (Italian) parsley

1 tablespoon chopped coriander (cilantro) leaves

55 g (2 oz/2/3 cup) fresh breadcrumbs

⅛ teaspoon ground saffron threads

Tomato sauce

400 g (14 oz) tin chopped tomatoes

1 onion, coarsely grated

1 tablespoon olive oil

2 garlic cloves, finely chopped

1 teaspoon paprika

½ teaspoon harissa (or ¼ teaspoon cayenne pepper), or to taste

½ teaspoon ground cumin

1 teaspoon sugar

1. Cut the fish fillets into rough pieces and put in a food processor, along with the egg, spring onion, parsley, coriander and breadcrumbs. Mix the saffron with 1 tablespoon warm water and add to the other ingredients with ¾ teaspoon salt and some freshly ground black pepper. Process to a thick paste, scraping down the side of the bowl occasionally.

2. With moistened hands, shape the fish mixture into balls the size of a walnut. Put on a tray, cover and set aside in the refrigerator.

3. Put the onion and olive oil in a saucepan and cook over medium heat for 2-3 minutes. Add the garlic, paprika, harissa or cayenne pepper and cumin. Stir for a few seconds, then add the chopped tomato, sugar, 250 ml (9 fl oz/1 cup) water and salt and freshly ground black pepper, to taste. Bring to the boil, cover and simmer for 8-10 minutes.

4. Add the fish balls to the tomato sauce, shaking the pan occasionally as they are added so that they settle into the sauce. Return to a gentle boil over medium heat, cover and simmer for 10-15 minutes. Serve the fish balls hot with crusty bread.

Radicchio and veal rolls

SERVES 4 ∗ **PREPARATION TIME: 15 MINUTES** ∗ **COOKING TIME: 10 MINUTES**

The sweetness of the balsamic vinegar offsets the sharpness of the radicchio. This is a great last-minute option for a special dinner. Use the best-quality balsamic vinegar you can find; it is worth the extra expense.

2 radicchio (red chicory)
olive oil spray for cooking
2 tablespoons balsamic vinegar
4 thin slices veal escalopes, each about 100 g (3½ oz)
40 g (1½ oz) freshly grated parmesan cheese

1. Trim the outer leaves from the radicchio and cut each head in half lengthways. Lightly spray oil in a large non-stick pan and fry the radicchio over a medium heat until lightly browned all over, 3–4 minutes. Season with salt and freshly ground black pepper and add 2 teaspoons of balsamic vinegar. Turn to coat, then remove from the pan.

2. Season the veal on both sides with salt and pepper and sprinkle parmesan cheese over one side. With the parmesan on the inside, wrap a slice of veal around the middle of each radicchio half, securing it in place with a toothpick.

3. Wipe the pan out with a paper towel. Lightly spray with oil and add the veal rolls. Brown quickly over medium–high heat, turning often. Add the remaining balsamic vinegar, cook for 5–6 seconds and remove from the heat. Turn the rolls to coat. Serve with the pan juices spooned over the top, accompanied by your favourite mash.

radicchio

With its beautiful deep red colour and mildly bitter taste, radicchio is a wonderfully simple way to spice up a basic salad. This vegetable resembles a red lettuce with elongated leaves. Its heart looks like a red Belgian endive, but the leaves are glossier. They can be shredded and used in pastas and stews, but it is when stirred through a risotto that they really come into their own. All types of radicchio can be stored in the fridge for several days and keep best wrapped in a damp tea towel. As with all leafy vegetables, it is best not to wash radicchio before storing, but to wait until you are ready to use it.

30 mins

Thai red squash curry

SERVES 4 * PREPARATION TIME: 15 MINUTES * COOKING TIME: 15 MINUTES

Thai cooking uses several kinds of curry pastes, each with a distinct flavour and colour obtained from its blend of herbs and spices. Red curry paste is highly fragrant. The commercial brands vary from medium to hot in intensity, so add more or less to suit your taste.

2 teaspoons oil
1–2 tablespoons Thai red curry paste
400 ml (14 fl oz) reduced fat coconut milk
2 tablespoons soy sauce
125 ml (4 fl oz/½ cup) light vegetable stock
2 teaspoons grated palm sugar
700 g (1 lb 9 oz) baby (pattypan) squash, halved, or quartered if large
100 g (3½ oz) baby corn, halved lengthways
100 g (3½ oz) mangetout (snow peas), topped and tailed
2 teaspoons lime juice
35 g (1¼ oz/⅓ cup) unsalted roasted cashews, coarsely chopped
lime wedges to serve (optional)

Note: If baby squash are unavailable, use courgettes (zucchini), cut into slices 2.5 cm (1 inch) thick.

1. Heat the oil in a large saucepan over medium–high heat and fry the curry paste for 1–2 minutes, or until the paste separates. Add the coconut milk, soy sauce, stock and palm sugar and stir until the sugar has melted. Bring to the boil.

2. Add the squash to the pan and return to the boil. Add the baby corn and simmer, covered, for 12–15 minutes, or until the squash is just tender. Add the snowpeas and lime juice and simmer, uncovered, for 1 minute. Serve with cashews scattered over the top, and accompanied by the lime wedges if desired.

baby squash

Baby (pattypan) squash are among the cutest members of the vegetable kingdom. These brightly coloured buttons of goodness belong to the marrow family, which also includes winter squash (pumpkins), cucumbers, melons, and gourds. Fresh and snappy when eaten raw, they are fabulously soft and luscious once cooked. With their subtle, sunny flavour, they are delicious with a dressing and lend themselves to a wide range of seasonings. Abundant throughout summer, they may be green and/or yellow in colour. Like all summer squash, the skin of baby squash is edible. Both the skin and flesh are firmer than those of other summer squash, however, which makes this squash good for baking and stewing.

desserts

These delicious dessert recipes are not tricky or fancy; they are all reliable, a few even very simple, and many welcomingly familiar, but with modern twists. Above all, they taste, smell and look wonderful and, most importantly, are low-fat. The emphasis is on fresh, good quality ingredients and classic dessert-making techniques to create dishes that can be cooked in under 30 minutes. When you glance through the desserts, you'll discover a tempting array of tasty ideas, making you want to delve in straight away. Even the names sound good — lime and coconut rice puddings, plum wine granita, aromatic peaches with sweetened Greek yoghurt and hazelnut crackle log.

Fruits feature in nearly all the recipes, as they are a deliciously healthy option also provide fantastic colour and flavour. With the abundance of tropical fruits available to us today, there is a fair dose of the tropical amongst these recipes, with desserts such as coconut pavlovas topped with tropical fruits and passionfruit cream, and mango and star anise sorbet with honey macadamia wafers doing their best to suggest languid days by the pool. Even dishes hailing from closer to home get in on the act — the traditional English dessert Eton mess goes tropical with the addition of red papaya and passionfruit. The wonderful thing about cooking with fruit is its versatility: it can make the familiar special — for example, the addition of reduced fat coconut milk and lime in a rice pudding; it can provide colour and also form wonderful desserts in its own right, like poached vanilla peaches with raspberry purée and passionfruit sauce.

There is a lightness and freshness to all of these desserts. They feature ingredients with the clean, tart citrus flavours of limes and lemons, the slight sharpness of yoghurt and the twist of exotic spices to give things a little bite and wake up the taste buds. Refreshing granitas and sorbets in shades of dusty pink and deep yellow make an appearance, as do tangy panna cottas and crispy nutty meringues.

It is amazing how the simple addition of some fruit, honey, nuts, liqueurs or spices such as cardamom and cinnamon can result in some truly memorable desserts.

30 mins

Vanilla soufflé with raspberry coulis

SERVES 6 ✳ **PREPARATION TIME: 10 MINUTES** ✳ **COOKING TIME: 20 MINUTES**

There is little more impressive (or utterly delicious) than a soufflé, puffed and hot from the oven. Unfortunately many cooks are too intimidated to attempt a soufflé at home — but really, they are not at all difficult to make,

40 g (1½ oz) low-fat spread
115 g (4 oz/½ cup) caster
  (superfine) sugar
250 ml (9 fl oz/1 cup) skimmed milk
1 teaspoon vanilla extract
1 vanilla bean, split lengthways
1 tablespoon plain (all-purpose) flour
4 eggs, separated
1 egg white
icing (confectioners') sugar
  for dusting

Raspberry coulis
400 g (14 oz) raspberries
80 g (2½ oz) icing (confectioners')
  sugar
lemon juice to taste

1. Preheat the oven 190°C (375°F/Gas 5). Use a double layer of non-stick baking paper to wrap around six 250 ml (9 fl oz/1 cup) soufflé dishes, making sure they extend 5 cm (2 in) above the rim. Secure the collars firmly by tying with kitchen string.

2. Melt 20 g (¾ oz) of low-fat spread and grease the soufflé dishes. Sprinkle each with a little of the caster sugar and turn dishes to coat the entire surface. Turn over and tap lightly to remove excess sugar.

3. Heat the milk, all but one tablespoon of the sugar, and the vanilla extract and vanilla bean in a small saucepan over low heat. Stir occasionally for 3–4 minutes, or until

the sugar has dissolved. Remove from the heat and set aside.

4. Melt the remaining low-fat spread in a saucepan over medium heat. Add the flour and stir until a smooth paste forms, then cook, stirring, for 1 minute. Remove from the heat and gradually whisk in the milk mixture. Return to the heat and cook, stirring constantly, until thick and smooth. Remove the vanilla bean and allow to cool.

5. Whisk the egg yolks, one at a time, into the vanilla mixture until combined. Whisk the egg whites in a bowl until stiff peaks form. Gradually add the remaining sugar, whisking continuously. Fold the meringue into the milk mixture. Spoon into the soufflé dishes and run a spoon around the tops about 2.5 cm (1 in) from the edge. Stand the soufflés in a roasting tin, then pour in enough hot water to come halfway up the sides of the dishes. Bake in the oven on the bottom shelf for 5 minutes. Reduce the heat to 180°C (350°F/Gas 4). Cook for a further 10–15 minutes, or until soufflé is risen.

6. Meanwhile, to make the coulis, blend or process the raspberries and sugar until a purée forms. Push the mixture through a sieve, discarding the solids, then add the lemon juice to taste. Dust the soufflés with icing sugar and serve with the coulis.

25 mins

Poached vanilla peaches with raspberry purée and passionfruit sauce

SERVES 4 ✳ PREPARATION TIME: 15 MINUTES ✳ COOKING TIME: 10 MINUTES

This delightful dessert is exactly what summer entertaining should be all about: a simple, quick recipe, full of flavour and colour, that utilizes the best of the season's produce and a tropical twist with the addition of passionfruit. You will need about three passionfruit for this recipe.

350 g (12 oz/1½ cups) caster (superfine) sugar
1 vanilla bean, halved lengthways
4 peaches
100 g (3½ oz/heaped ¾ cup) fresh raspberries or frozen raspberries, thawed
4 small scoops reduced fat vanilla ice cream

Passionfruit sauce
60 ml (2 fl oz/¼ cup) passionfruit pulp
2 tablespoons caster (superfine) sugar

1. Put the sugar, vanilla bean and 625 ml (21½ fl oz/2½ cups) of water in a large saucepan. Stir over low heat until the sugar has dissolved. Bring to a slow boil, then add the peaches and simmer for 5 minutes, or until the peaches are just tender and softened. Cool the peaches in the syrup, then remove with a slotted spoon. Peel and halve the peaches, removing the stones.

2. Put the raspberries in a food processor and process until puréed. Push the raspberries through a sieve, discarding the pulp.

3. To make the passionfruit sauce, combine the passionfruit pulp with the sugar and stir until the sugar has dissolved.

4. To serve, divide the raspberry purée among 4 glasses. Arrange a scoop of ice cream and two peach halves on top. Spoon over the passionfruit sauce and serve immediately.

peach

This fragrant, juicy stone fruit is instantly recognizable by its rosy pink, downy skin. Inside, the flesh of the peach may be yellow or white, separating easily from the stone (freestone) or not (clingstone). Peaches do not last long, so buy only as many as can be eaten or cooked within the space of three to four days. Avoid bruised or soft peaches; the latter will taste floury and be sadly disappointing. Apart from enjoying their succulent flesh just as it is, peaches are excellent for poaching in wine or syrup and for using in tarts, sorbets and sauces.

30 mins

Pears in red wine

SERVES 6 ∗ **PREPARATION TIME: 10 MINUTES** ∗ **COOKING TIME: 20 MINUTES**

Simple, but impossible to improve upon, this dessert is yet another timeless favourite from the French dessert repertoire. Select firm but ripe pears of similar size so they all cook to tenderness at the same time and, if desired, use an apple corer to remove the core before poaching.

1 tablespoon arrowroot
750 ml (26 gl oz/3 cups) red wine
110 g (3¾ oz) sugar
1 stick cinnamon
6 cloves
1 tablespoons grated orange zest
1 tablespoons grated lemon zest
6 pears (ripe but still firm)

1. Mix the arrowroot with 2 tablespoons of the wine and set aside. Heat the remaining wine in a saucepan with the sugar, cinnamon stick, cloves and orange and lemon zest. Simmer gently for a few minutes, stirring occasionally, until the sugar has dissolved.

2. Peel the pears, but don't remove the stalks. Put the whole pears in the saucepan of wine, cover and poach gently for 15-20 minutes, or until they are very tender, turning occasionally. Lift out with a slotted spoon and place on serving plates.

3. Strain the wine mixture, discarding solids, then pour back into the saucepan. Stir the arrowroot mixture and add to the hot wine. Simmer gently, stirring occasionally, until thickened. Pour over the pears and stand until cooled. Serve with half fat crème fraîche.

pear

Pears reached their zenith of popularity in seventeenth century France where they were considered the most regal of fruits. King Louis XIV had much to do with this; he adored pears and many a noble found favour at his court by developing some new variety for his enjoyment. Indeed, the French are responsible for some of the varieties we know and most love today. The perfect pear for this recipe is the conference. Peel away the greenish-brown skin and discover the firm, creamy, and aromatic flesh which keeps its shape extremely well when cooked. Or use the diminutive corella pear (pictured), which also has excellent flavour.

Mini pavlovas with tropical fruits and coconut passionfruit cream

SERVES 4 * **PREPARATION TIME: 10 MINUTES** * **COOKING TIME: NIL**

Who doesn't get excited by a crisp meringue base, laden with cream and fresh fruit? Use passionfruit, lychees and papaya to give a traditional cream topping a tropical twist. However, any seasonal fresh fruit can be used.

Passionfruit cream
250 g (9 oz/1 cup) half fat
   crème fraîche
2 tablespoons icing (confectioners')
   sugar
15 g (½ oz/¼ cup) shredded coconut
4 passionfruit

½ small red papaya, seeded
   and peeled
4 fresh lychees, halved and seeded
½ mango, peeled and seeded
4 ready-made meringue nests

Note: For a quick alternative, top
the meringue nests with half fat
crème fraîche, a selection of fresh
berries and a quick coulis made
from puréed and sieved berries.

1. To make the coconut passionfruit cream, combine the crème fraîche and icing sugar together until smooth. Fold the coconut and passionfruit pulp through the cream and refrigerate until ready to serve.

2. Cut the papaya, lychees and mango into very small dice. To serve, top the ready-made meringue nests with some of the passionfruit cream and accompany with the diced fruit.

Three ways with fresh fruit

In every Moroccan household, the main meal is completed with fresh fruit, either picked from courtyard fruit trees or bought at the souk. At banquets, beautifully arranged platters of fresh fruit, often nestled in ice, celebrate the season. When fruit is prepared, it could be scented with flower water, dusted with cinnamon, crowned with chopped nuts — a visual and sensory delight and the perfect finale to a meal.

Watermelon with rosewater and mint
SERVES 4 ∗ **PREPARATION TIME: 10 MINUTES** ∗ **COOKING TIME: NIL**
Wipe the skin of a 1.5 kg (3 lb 5 oz) piece of watermelon with a clean, damp cloth. Working over a plate to catch any juice, remove the skin and cut the watermelon into 3 cm (1¼ in) cubes, removing any visible seeds. Pile the cubes in a bowl or on a platter. Pour the watermelon juice into a small jug and stir in 3 teaspoons rosewater. Sprinkle over the watermelon, cover and chill in the refrigerator for 1 hour, or until required. Scatter with small fresh mint leaves and serve chilled.

Peaches with sugar and cinnamon
SERVES 4 ∗ **PREPARATION TIME: 10 MINUTES** ∗ **COOKING TIME: NIL**
Peel 6 freestone peaches. To do this, cut around each peach following the groove on the side of the peach. Put the peaches in a bowl of boiling water for 1 minute, then plunge them into a bowl of cold water to cool. Remove from the water and peel the skin away — it should slip off easily. Separate the peach halves with a gentle twist and remove the stones. Brush the cut surfaces lightly with lemon juice. Sit the peach halves on a bed of crushed ice in a large, shallow bowl. Crush 4 sugar cubes, sprinkle on each peach half and dust lightly with ground cinnamon.

Bananas with yoghurt
SERVES 4 ∗ **PREPARATION TIME: 10 MINUTES** ∗ **COOKING TIME: 5 MINUTES**
Slice 4–5 large bananas at an angle to give longish ovals of banana about 4 cm (1½ in) thick. Arrange in overlapping circles in a round, shallow dish. Mix 60 ml (2 fl oz/¼ cup) fresh orange juice with 3 teaspoons orange flower water and sprinkle over the banana. Mix 250 g (9 oz/1 cup) thick low-fat Greek-style yoghurt with 2 tablespoons honey and pile in the centre of the banana. Lightly roast and chop 60 g (2¼ oz/½ cup) walnut pieces and sprinkle over the yoghurt and bananas. Drizzle 1 tablespoon thick honey over the walnuts.

Almond and rosewater puddings with orange and date salad

SERVES 4 ∗ **PREPARATION TIME: 15 MINUTES + SETTING TIME**
COOKING TIME: 10 MINUTES

These pretty puddings contain almond aroma, which is available from some delicatessens. It is preferable to almond extract; however, ¼ teaspoon of almond extract can be used successfully, if necessary.

3 teaspoons powdered gelatine
500 ml (17 fl oz/2 cups)
skimmed milk
2 tablespoons caster (superfine)
sugar
½ teaspoon bitter almond aroma
1 teaspoon rosewater
2 oranges
8 fresh dates, pitted and roughly
chopped

Strain the warm milk and gelatine mixture into a bowl.

Peel the orange and slice in between the membrane, avoiding any white pith.

1. Put 60 ml (2 fl oz/¼ cup) of water in a small bowl and sprinkle with the gelatine. Leave the gelatine to sponge and swell. Stir the milk and sugar in a small saucepan over medium heat until the sugar has dissolved. When the milk reaches lukewarm, remove the saucepan from the heat. Continue stirring while you add the gelatine mixture and stir until it has dissolved into the warm milk. Strain into a bowl, then stir in the almond aroma and rosewater.

2. Pour the mixture into 4 x 125 ml (4 fl oz/½ cup) dariole moulds and refrigerate for at least 3 hours, or until firm.

3. Remove the skin and pith from the oranges with a sharp knife. Holding the oranges over a bowl, remove the segments by slicing in between the membrane. Remove any seeds. Add the segments to the bowl with the juice. Squeeze any remaining juice from the orange skeletons. Add the chopped dates to the bowl and toss to combine.

4. To serve, wrap the dariole moulds in a hot, clean dish cloth and invert the puddings onto plates. Accompany the puddings with the orange and date salad.

Lime and coconut rice puddings

SERVES 4 * **PREPARATION TIME: 10 MINUTES** * **COOKING TIME: 20 MINUTES**

It's no accident that limes and coconuts grow in similar parts of the world: their flavours complement each other perfectly. The sharpness of lime means it is often used as a flavour enhancer, and here it nicely cuts through the richness of the coconut milk.

500 ml (14 fl oz) skimmed milk

500 ml (21 fl oz) reduced fat coconut milk

1 lime, zest finely grated

60 ml (2 fl oz/¼ cup) lime juice

3 kaffir lime (makrut) leaves, halved

140 g (5 oz/⅔ cup) medium-grain rice

100 g (3½ oz/¾ cup) shaved palm sugar (jaggery) or 100 g (3½ oz/½ cup) soft brown sugar

toasted shredded coconut for decoration, optional

1. Put the milk, coconut milk, lime zest, lime juice and lime leaves in a large saucepan and bring to the boil. Add the rice and stir to combine. Reduce the heat to low and simmer, stirring occasionally, for 20-25 minutes, or until the rice is tender.

2. Remove the saucepan from the heat and add the palm sugar, stirring until it has dissolved and the mixture is creamy.

3. Remove the lime leaves and divide the rice pudding among 4 x 250 ml (9 fl oz/1 cup) capacity heatproof glasses or ramekins. Serve warm or cold, decorated with shredded coconut, if using.

coconut

The coconut tree and its fruit have been appreciated for centuries. Its uses range from supplying material for thatching and weaving to providing a nutritious and refreshing drink — complete with its own cup. When not quite ripe, coconut flesh is soft and jelly-like and the juice sweet and watery. As the coconut ripens, the flesh hardens and the amount of juice decreases. This juice is quite different from coconut milk and cream, which are produced by soaking grated coconut flesh in boiling water and squeezing out the resulting liquid. Other products include copra, which is dried coconut flesh; coconut oil, which is made from copra; desiccated coconut; and coconut liqueur.

Vanilla buttermilk panna cotta with summer fruits

SERVES 4 ∗ **PREPARATION TIME: 10 MINUTES + SETTING TIME**
COOKING TIME: 5 MINUTES

Its name seems to suggest otherwise, but buttermilk is actually made from skimmed milk and is lower in fat than full-cream milk. An acid-producing bacteria is added to the milk, thickening it and giving it a tangy flavour. It goes perfectly in this panna cotta, producing a smooth, creamy dessert.

Panna cotta
2 teaspoons powdered gelatine
**100 ml (3 ½ fl oz) cream
(whipping)**
**55 g (2 oz/¼ cup) caster (superfine)
sugar**
½ vanilla bean, split lengthways
250 ml (9 fl oz/1 cup) buttermilk
**150 g (5 ½ oz) low-fat Greek-style
yoghurt**

2 passionfruit
**2 teaspoons caster (superfine)
sugar**
**½ small pineapple, peeled and
cored**
**½ small red papaya, seeded and
peeled**

1. To make the panna cotta, lightly grease 4 x 125 ml (4 fl oz/½ cup) metal, glass or ceramic moulds.

2. Put 2 teaspoons of water in a small bowl and sprinkle with the gelatine. Leave the gelatine to sponge and swell. Put the cream, sugar and vanilla bean in a small saucepan and stir over low heat for 2–3 minutes, or until the sugar has dissolved.

3. Whisk the gelatine mixture into the cream mixture until the gelatine has dissolved. Set aside to infuse for 3 minutes.

4. Scrape the seeds from the vanilla bean into the cream mixture, discarding the vanilla pod. Pour the mixture into a bowl. Shake the buttermilk carton well before measuring, then whisk the buttermilk and yoghurt into the cream mixture. Divide the mixture among the prepared moulds. Put the moulds on a tray, cover with plastic wrap and refrigerate for 3–4 hours, or until set.

5. Sieve the passionfruit pulp into a small bowl, discarding the seeds. Stir in the sugar. Cut the pineapple and papaya into long thin slivers.

6. To serve, gently run a small knife around the side of each mould and turn the panna cotta out onto large serving plates. If they don't readily come out, briefly dip the moulds in a bowl of hot water. Arrange the fruit slivers around the panna cotta and drizzle with the passionfruit juice.

**Remove the papaya
seeds using a spoon.**

**Divide the panna cotta
mixture among the
moulds.**

30 mins

Apple and passionfruit crumble

SERVES 6 ✳ **PREPARATION TIME: 10 MINUTES** ✳ **COOKING TIME: 20 MINUTES**

There are countless versions of the fruit crumble but all rely on the winning formula of sweetened fruit covered by a golden topping of flour, sugar and butter. Here, passionfruit and shredded coconut add a little complexity to the basic flavours.

4 passionfruit
4 green apples
55 g (2 oz/¼ cup) caster (superfine) sugar, plus 80 g (2¾ oz/⅓ cup)
60 g (2¼ oz/1 cup) shredded coconut
90 g (3¼ oz/¾ cup) plain (all-purpose) flour
50 g (1 ¾ oz) low-fat spread, softened

1. Preheat the oven to 180°C (350°F/Gas 4) and grease a 1 litre (35 fl oz/4 cup) ovenproof dish.

2. Sieve the passionfruit, discarding the pulp, and place the juice in a bowl. Peel, core and thinly slice the apples and add to the passionfruit juice, along with the 55 g (2 oz/¼ cup) of sugar. Mix well, then transfer the mixture to the prepared dish.

3. Combine the shredded coconut, flour, extra sugar and butter in a bowl and rub together until the mixture has a crumble texture. Pile on top of the apple mixture.

4. Bake the crumble for 20-25 minutes, or until the topping is crisp and golden.

Make sure you squeeze out as much juice as possible.

Use your fingertips to rub the butter into the dry ingredients.

Three ways with figs

One of the pleasures of late summer through autumn would have to be eating fresh figs, plump, purple and luscious.

Figs with rosewater, almonds and honey

SERVES 6 * **PREPARATION TIME: 10 MINUTES** * **COOKING TIME: NIL**

Wash 12 fresh purple-skinned figs gently and pat them dry with paper towels. Cut each fig into quarters, starting from the stem end and cutting almost to the base, then gently open out and put on a serving platter. Cover and chill in the refrigerator for 1 hour, or until required. Coarsely chop 50 g (1¾ oz/⅓ cup) lightly roasted blanched almonds. Carefully dribble about ¼ teaspoon rosewater onto the exposed centre of each fig, and sprinkle 1 teaspoon of the chopped almonds into each fig. Drizzle 1–2 tablespoons honey over the nuts. Serve immediately.

Poached figs with almonds and spices

SERVES 4–6 * **PREPARATION TIME: 10 MINUTES** * **COOKING TIME: 20 MINUTES**

Take 250 g (9 oz/1 cup) ready-to-eat dried figs and insert a blanched almond into each fig from the base. Wrap 3 cloves, 3 bruised cardamom pods and ½ teaspoon black peppercorns in a piece of muslin and tie securely. Add 115 g (4 oz/½ cup) sugar to a saucepan with 200 ml (7 fl oz) of water and cook over medium heat, stirring, until the sugar has dissolved. Bring to the boil, add the bag of spices, the thinly peeled zest of ½ lemon, 1 cinnamon stick and the figs. Return to the boil, then reduce the heat and simmer for 15 minutes, or until tender. Transfer the figs to a serving dish with a slotted spoon and strain the syrup over them. Serve warm or chilled with thick yoghurt.

Figs with honeyed yoghurt

SERVES 4–6 * **PREPARATION TIME: 30 MINUTES** * **COOKING TIME: NIL**

Gently wash 12 fresh figs and dry gently with paper towels. Chill for 25 minutes. Mix 250 g (9 oz/1 cup) thick low-fat Greek-style yoghurt with 2 tablespoons honey. Coarsely chop 2 tablespoons pistachio nuts and set aside. Cut each fig into quarters, starting from the stem end and cutting almost to the base. Gently open each fig and place on a flat serving dish. Dribble ¼ teaspoon orange flower water over the exposed centre of each fig and pile about 1 tablespoon of the yoghurt into each. Drizzle 1 teaspoon honey on top of the yoghurt in each fig and sprinkle with the chopped pistachios.

Mango and star anise sorbet with honey macadamia wafers

SERVES 6 ∗ **PREPARATION TIME: 15 MINUTES + FREEZING TIME**
COOKING TIME: 15 MINUTES

Use the honey macadamia wafers as spoons for scooping up this summer sorbet: smooth, gently perfumed sorbet against sweet, nutty crunchiness. Perfect. Star anise will bring a subtle aniseed flavour to the sorbet.

185 g (6½ oz/heaped ¾ cup) caster (superfine) sugar
2 star anise
1 tablespoon lemon juice
3 mangoes, flesh chopped to give 500 g (1 lb 2 oz)
1 egg white, at room temperature

Honey macadamia wafers
1 egg white, at room temperature
60 g (2¼ oz/¼ cup) caster (superfine) sugar
2 tablespoons honey
2 tablespoons plain (all-purpose) flour, sifted
40 g (1½ oz) unsalted butter, melted and cooled
100 g (3½ oz/¾ cup) chopped macadamia nuts

1. Combine the sugar with 310 ml (10¾ fl oz/1¼ cups) of water and the star anise in a saucepan. Stir over medium heat until the sugar has dissolved. Bring to the boil, then reduce the heat and simmer for 1 minute. Set aside to cool to room temperature. Stir in the lemon juice.

2. Put the mango in a food processor and purée until smooth. Strain the sugar syrup onto the mango and process until just combined, then transfer to a shallow metal container, cover and freeze. When the sorbet is three-quarters frozen, transfer it to a food processor, add the egg white and blend until smooth. Return the sorbet to the container and freeze until required.

3. To make the honey macadamia wafers, preheat the oven to 200°C (400°F/Gas 6). Line two 30 cm (12 inch) square baking trays with baking paper. Put the egg white in a small bowl and beat with electric beaters until soft peaks form. Gradually add the sugar and continue beating until the sugar has dissolved. Beat in the honey and then fold in the flour and butter. Spread the mixture very thinly over the prepared trays, then sprinkle evenly with the macadamia nuts. Bake for 7–10 minutes, or until lightly golden. Set aside to cool on the trays, then break into pieces. Store in an airtight container as the wafers will soften on standing. Serve scoops of mango sorbet accompanied by large pieces of the honey macadamia wafers.

Strain the star anise syrup onto the mango purée.

Sprinkle the macadamia nuts in an even layer.

Tropical Eton mess

SERVES 4 * **PREPARATION TIME: 15 MINUTES** * **COOKING TIME: NIL**

This dessert makes no pretence of sophistication, which means it will be a sure-fire winner with everyone. The fruit can be changed to match the season, though stick with fruit that are juicy but firm — you don't want a mushy mess. If you change the fruit, select complementary liqueurs.

4 ready-made meringue nests
125 g (4½ oz/heaped ¾ cup) strawberries, thickly sliced
½ small red papaya, seeded, peeled and cubed
4 passionfruit
1 tablespoon caster (superfine) sugar
1 tablespoon raspberry liqueur, such as Framboise, or orange liqueur, such as Grand Marnier, optional
175 g (6 oz/¾ cup) half fat crème fraîche
175 g (6 oz/¾ cup) low-fat Greek-style yoghurt

1. Roughly crumble the meringues.

2. Combine the strawberries, papaya and half the passionfruit pulp in a bowl. Stir in the sugar and the liqueur, if using. Set aside for 5 minutes, or until ready to assemble.

3. Just before serving, combine the crème fraîche and yoghurt together, stirring until smooth. Add the fruit mixture all at once and stir until roughly combined. Spoon half the mixture into 4 x 310 ml (10¾ fl oz/1¼ cup) tall parfait glasses. Top with the crumbled meringue and then the remaining fruit. Garnish with the remaining passionfruit pulp and serve immediately.

15 mins

Peaches with sweetened Greek yoghurt

SERVES 4 ✻ **PREPARATION TIME: 10 MINUTES + MACERATING TIME**
COOKING TIME: 5 MINUTES

This fragrant, heady dessert infuses peaches with four different spices — a delectable dish taking full advantage of the season's stone fruits. Macerate the peaches in the syrup for no longer than 4 hours or the peaches will discolour and lose their beautiful blush.

225 g (8 oz/1 cup) caster (superfine) sugar
1 vanilla bean, split lengthways
1 cinnamon stick
6 cardamom pods
2 star anise
4 peaches
2 tablespoons dark brown sugar
300 g (10½ oz/1¼ cups) low-fat Greek-style yoghurt

1. Pour 500 ml (17 fl oz/2 cups) of water into a saucepan and add the caster sugar. Heat over medium heat until the sugar has dissolved. Scrape the seeds from the vanilla bean into the saucepan and add the pod, cinnamon stick, cardamom pods and star anise. Boil for 2 minutes, then set aside to cool.

2. Put the peaches in a heatproof bowl and cover with boiling water. Set aside for 1 minute, then drain the peaches and refresh in ice-cold water. Halve the peaches, removing the stones and skin. Working quickly to prevent the peaches from browning, place the peaches in a bowl and strain the cooled syrup over them. Refrigerate for several hours to allow the peaches to macerate in the syrup.

3. Stir the dark brown sugar through the yoghurt and serve with the peaches and syrup.

Infuse the syrup with the aromatic spices.

Soak the peaches in boiling water to make them easy to peel.

20 mins

Plum wine granita

SERVES 6 ✳ **PREPARATION TIME: 10 MINUTES + FREEZING TIME**
COOKING TIME: 10 MINUTES

For a refreshing close to a sophisticated dinner on a hot summer evening, this granita is an ideal choice. Fruity, with a tart sweetness and a hint of ginger, as well as lightly alcoholic, this bright dessert makes a beautiful presentation.

115 g (4 oz/½ cup) caster
   (superfine) sugar
a few strips lemon zest
2 cm (¾ in) piece young fresh
   ginger, thinly sliced
500 g (1 lb 2 oz) ripe plums, seeded
500 ml (17 fl oz/2 cups) Japanese
   plum wine

Note: Plum wine is avaiable from Asian grocers, Japanese grocers and good supermarkets.

1. Combine the sugar with the lemon zest, ginger and 375 ml (13 fl oz/1½ cups) water. Stir over high heat until the sugar has dissolved, then bring to the boil. Reduce the heat to low and simmer for 10 minutes. Cool completely, then strain.

2. Purée the plum flesh in a food processor, then strain through a fine sieve to extract the juice — you will need about 250 ml (9 fl oz/1 cup). Add to the cooled syrup with the plum wine, then pour into a shallow 30 x 20 cm (12 x 8 in) metal container. Place in the freezer until the mixture begins to freeze around the edges.

3. Remove from the freezer and scrape the frozen sections back into the mixture with a fork. Repeat every 30 minutes, until the mixture has even-sized ice crystals. Just before serving, beat the mixture with a fork, then spoon into six bowls or glasses.

umeshu

Umeshu is commonly called 'plum wine' in English, but technically it is neither wine nor precisely of plums. The ume is really a kind of apricot. Due to its high acidity, it is not eaten raw, but in early summer the green fruits are ready to be made into a delightful liqueur. Although produced commercially, umeshu is also popularly made at home. Layered with rock sugar, and immersed in white liquor, the fruit is left to macerate and ferment in a cool, dark place. In 3 months it is ready to drink and, imbibed as an aperitif, is considered very beneficial to the health. This traditional liqueur is sometimes used to create contemporary cocktails and some desserts.

Crêpes suzette

SERVES 6 ✳ **PREPARATION TIME: 10 MINUTES** ✳ **COOKING TIME: 10 MINUTES**

Crêpes are fun to cook — just make sure you use a frying pan with a non-stick surface to avoid the frustration of torn crêpes, and allow yourself to make a few less-than-perfect specimens until you get into a good swirling/flipping rhythm.

250 g (9 oz/2 cups) plain
   (all-purpose) flour
a pinch salt
1 teaspoon sugar
2 eggs, lightly beaten
400 ml (14 fl oz) skimmed milk
20 g (¾ oz) low-fat spread, melted
2 tablespoons grated orange zest
1 tablespoon grated lemon zest
oil spray for frying

125 g (4½ oz) caster (superfine)
   sugar
250 ml (9 fl oz/1 cup) orange juice
1 tablespoon grated orange zest
2 tablespoons brandy or Cognac
2 tablespoons Grand Marnier

1. Sift the flour, salt and sugar into a bowl and make a well in the centre. Mix the eggs and milk together with 100 ml (3½ fl oz) of water and pour slowly into the well, whisking until a smooth batter forms. Stir in the melted butter. Cover and refrigerate for 20 minutes. Stir the orange and lemon zest into the crêpe batter.

2. Heat and lightly grease a crêpe pan. Pour in just enough batter to coat the base of the pan in a thin even layer, pouring out any excess. Cook over medium heat for about 1 minute, or until the crêpe starts to come away from the side of the pan. Turn the crêpe and cook on the other side for 1 minute, or until light golden. Repeat with the remaining batter. Fold the crêpes into quarters.

3. Melt the sugar in a large frying pan over low heat and cook to a caramel, tilting the pan so the caramel browns evenly. Pour in the orange juice and zest and boil for 2 minutes. Put the crêpes in the pan and spoon the sauce over them.

4. Add the brandy and Grand Marnier and flambé by lighting the pan with your gas flame or a match (stand well back when you do this and keep a pan lid handy for emergencies). Add the butter and swirl the pan until it melts. Serve immediately

Caramel will spit when the juice is added so take great care.

Swirl the pan to combine the butter with the syrup.

Hazelnut crackle log

SERVES 6–8 ＊ **PREPARATION TIME: 10 MINUTES** ＊ **COOKING TIME: 20 MINUTES**

Early forms of meringue were called 'sugar puff', and it is not hard to see why. Crisp and crackly, the appeal of meringue comes as much from its texture as its taste. This meringue isn't as sweet as some, due to the hazelnuts, which combine wonderfully with the coffee mascarpone filling.

Meringue
70 g (2½ oz/½ cup) roasted
   skinned hazelnuts
4 egg whites, at room temperature
150 g (5½ oz/2/3 cup) caster
   (superfine) sugar
1 teaspoon cornflour (cornstarch)
1 teaspoon natural vanilla extract
1 teaspoon white wine vinegar

Filling
2 teaspoons instant coffee granules
2 teaspoons hot water
200 g (7 oz) light cream cheese
   or quark
2 tablespoons icing (confectioners')
   sugar, sifted

Spread the mixture evenly using a palette knife.

Spread the filling to cover the whole meringue.

1. To make the meringue, preheat the oven to 150°C (300°F/Gas 2). Draw a 20 x 35 cm (8 x 14 inch) rectangle on a sheet of baking paper. Put the sheet, pencil side down, on a baking tray.

2. Put the hazelnuts in a food processor and process until the nuts are coarsely ground. Whisk the egg whites in a large bowl until soft peaks form. Gradually add the sugar, 1 tablespoon at a time, and whisk until stiff and glossy. Gently fold in the hazelnuts, then the cornflour, vanilla and vinegar. Spoon onto the baking tray and spread evenly inside the marked rectangle. Bake for 20-25 minutes, or until the meringue is set and lightly golden.

3. Lay a large sheet of baking paper on a work surface and invert the cooked meringue on top. Peel off the baking paper and set aside to cool for 15 minutes.

4. To make the filling, dissolve the instant coffee in the hot water. Put the coffee, cream cheese or quark and icing sugar in a bowl and mix well.

5. Spread the filling evenly over the meringue. Starting at one short end and using the baking paper as a lever, gently roll up the meringue. The outer surface will crack into a pattern. Serve immediately, cut into slices.

index

A READER'S DIGEST BOOK

Published by The Reader's Digest Association Limited
11 Westferry Circus
Canary Wharf
London E14 4HE
www.readersdigest.co.uk

We are committed to both the quality of our products and the service we
provide to our customers. We value your comments, so please feel free to
call us on 08705 113366, or via our website at www.readersdigest.co.uk.
If you have any comments about the content of any of your books, you can
contact us at bgeditorial@readersdigest.co.uk

This book was designed, edited and produced by Murdoch Books Pty Limited.

Series Food Editor: Fiona Roberts
Designer: Joanna Byrne
Design Concept: Uber Creative
Production: Kita George

Printed by Midas Printing (Asia) Ltd. PRINTED IN CHINA.

IMPORTANT: Those who might be at risk from the effects of salmonella
poisoning (the elderly, pregnant women, young children and those suffering
from immune deficiency diseases) should consult their doctor with any
concerns about eating raw eggs.

CONVERSION GUIDE: You may find cooking times vary depending on the
oven you are using. For fan-assisted ovens, as a general rule, set the oven
temperature to 20°C (35°F) lower than indicated in the recipe. We have used
20 ml (4 teaspoon) tablespoon measures. If you are using a 15 ml (3 teaspoon)
tablespoon for most recipes the difference will not be noticeable.

Book code: 410-706 UP0000-1
ISBN: 978 0 276 44253 7
Oracle code: 250011416H